Smith County
Tennessee

BIBLE AND TOMBSTONE RECORDS WITH SOME CHURCH MINUTES

WPA RECORDS

Heritage Books
2024

HERITAGE BOOKS

AN IMPRINT OF HERITAGE BOOKS, INC.

Books, CDs, and more—Worldwide

For our listing of thousands of titles see our website
at
www.HeritageBooks.com

A Facsimile Reprint
Published 2024 by
HERITAGE BOOKS, INC.
Publishing Division
5810 Ruatan Street
Berwyn Heights, MD 20740

Originally published
October 1, 1938

International Standard Book Number
Paperbound: 978-0-7884-8769-9

PREFACE

This material is taken from the 1938 W. P. A. transcription. The index page numbers are given with a circle around a number in the upper right hand corner of each page. These may differ from the typed number. There is only one listing of a name per page so the reader is advised to search each page closely. When women are indexed sometimes they are listed under both their surname and their married name. Carefully look for these.

TENNESSEE

SMITH COUNTY

BIBLE & TOMBSTONE RECORDS

HISTORICAL RECORDS PROJECT
Official Project No. 465-44-3-115

COPIED UNDER WORKS PROGRESS ADMINISTRATION

MRS. JOHN TROTWOOD MOORE
STATE LIBRARIAN & ARCHIVIST SPONSOR

MRS. ELIZABETH D. COPPEDGE
DIRECTOR OF WOMEN'S & PROFESSIONAL PROJECTS

MRS. PENELOPE JOHNSON ALLEN
STATE SUPERVISOR

MISS MATILDA A. PORTER
DISTRICT SUPERVISOR

Copied

by

MRS. BESSIE GIBBS
MRS. CORA WHITEFIELD
MISS HATTIE WINFRIE
MISS REBECCA BALLENGER
MISS MATTIE M. JONES

OCTOBER 1, 1938

SMITH COUNTY

BIBLE AND TOMBSTONE RECORDS

CONTENTS

INDEX IN BACK

BIBLE RECORDS

TOMBSTONE INSCRIPTIONS

BIBLE - RECORDS

AGEE FAMILY BIBLE
SMITH COUNTY

Record from the Bible of Jonathan Agee, descendant of Mathew
Agee, of France, came from Virginia to Smith County. This
Bible was printed in 1838, by C. Alexander & Co.,Anthenians
Building, Franklin Place, Philadelphia, Pa.
First owner: Jonathan Agee, Gordonsville, Tennessee.
Second owner: Mrs. Mary Griffith,(his daughter),Marion, Ky.
Present owner: Edd Agee, Gordonsville, Tennessee.
Information obtained from Edd Agee, Gordonsville, Tenn.
Copied by Mrs. Bessie Gibbs, Carthage, Tennessee.
December 30, 1936.

Jonathan Agee,
Born Jan. 19, 1789.

Ephraim Agee,
Born May 20, 1800.

William Agee,
Born Jan. 3, 1811.

Jonathan W. Agee,
Born Feb. 27, 1813.

Malinda Agee,
Was born Nov. 25, 1815.

Sarah Agee,
Died Dec. 20, 1856.

Jonathan Agee,
Died Apr. 5, 1859.

Jonathan Agee & Sara
Williams, was married,
August 25, 1808.

Aaron F. Griffith &
Mary J. Agee,married
Nov. 14, 1867.Crittenden
County, Ky.

James Agee,
Was born April 1, 1818.

Daniel Bethel Agee,
Was born Sept. 28, 1820.

Jeremiah Agee,
Was born Feb. 18, 1823.

Mary Jane Agee,
Was born Aug. 26, 1825.

Sarah Ann Agee,
Was born Dec. 11, 1827.

Jeremiah Agee & Elizabeth
Agee was married,
Dec. 21, 1843.

Jeremiah Agee,
Was born Feb. 18, 1823.

Elizabeth Agee,
Was born Oct. 5, 1824.

John D. Agee,
Was born July 8, 1845.

Martha Jane Agee,
Was born March 7, 1848.

William S. Agee,
Was born Oct. 18, 1850.

(Agee Family Bible p. 2.)

Lion Taylor Agee,
Was born Oct. 5, 1853.

Joel W. Agee,
Was born Dec. 27, 1856.

Mary Elizabeth Agee,
Was born Feb. 13, 1859.

Jeremiah Edwin Agee,
Was born March 3, 1867.

SMITH COUNTY

ROBERT ALLEN - BIBLE RECORD

Records from the family Bible of Robert Allen, of
"Greenwood", Smith County, Tennessee.
This Bible was printed by Mathew Carey, No. 122 Market Street,
Philadelphia, Penn. Nov. 7, 1803.
It is now the property of Mrs. George B. Kirkpatrick,
Richland Ave., Nashville, Tenn.
Copied by Miss Matilda A. Porter, June, 1936.

MARRIAGES

Robert Allen was married to Rebecca Greer
the 28 of December 1803

Robert Allen and Alethia Van Horn married
March 3, 1825, in the City of Washington, by the
Rev. Mr. Post.

George C. Allen & Martha Overton married
Oct. 27, 1842 at her fathers near Nashville.

Andrew Allison was married to Rebecca G.
Allen, daughter of Robert and Rebecca
on the 24th May 1832 at Greenwood by
Rev. Samuel C. McConnell.

Dixon Allen, son of Robert & Rebecca Allen
was married in Nashville to Mrs. Louisa W. Gibbs
on the 26 day of Sept 1832.

Joseph W. Allen & Catherine K. Maxwell married
in Jonesboro E. Tenn. on Thursday evening the
4th of April 1839, by the Rev. J. W. Cunningham.

Joseph W. Allen and Mrs. Mary Hemphill (Bently)
were married in Bledsoe County, Tenn. Thursday
August 24th 1854 by Rev. Iran W. Klegg.

Virginia D. Allen and Thomas P. Bridges
married at Carthage Tenn., by Rev. John Nichols,
on Wednesday, February 4, 1880

(Robert Allen - Bible Record p. 2)

BIRTHS

Robert Allen was born June 19 Anno Domini 1778.

Rebecca Allen wife of Robert Allen was born 22 of August, Anno Domini 1787.

Alethia Van Horn (second wife of Robert Allen) was born in Prince George County Maryland on the 18th of Oct. 1804.

Robert & Rebecca's daughter, Eliza Allen, was born Oct. 11, Thursday evening, 9 oclock Anno Domini 1804.

James Greer Allen was born, Wednesday, 2 oclock, March 5, 1806.

Tilman Dixon Allen was born the 2nd Day of March in the year A.D. 1808

Caroline Walton Allen born February the 11th 1810

Rebecca Greer Allen born the 24th day of February A. D. 1812

Joseph Webster Allen was born the 16th day of May A.D. 1814

Robert Allen was born July, 13, 1816, son of Robert and Rebecca.

George Campbell Allen was born the 30th day of September 1818, son of Robert and Rebecca.

Archibald Van Horn Allen son of Robert Allen and Alethia Van Horn was born May 21, 1827 on Monday Morning at Greenwood.

David Burford Allen was born January 3, 1830, at Greenwood.

William Rozin Allen was born 15 March 1833, at Greenwood.

Alethia Beale Allen was born 3d of June 1835 at Greenwood.

John Allen was born at Greenwood on the 22d of April in the year A.D. 1837.

Eliza Clarisa Allen born at Greenwood the 24 August 1839

Virginia Dixon Allen was born at Greenwood Monday morning at 9 oclock July 10 A.D. 1843

Mary Webster Lucas, sister of Robert Allen, was born Aug. 22, 1797.

DEATHS

Departed this life in the 61 year of his age on the 4th day of November
1811, George Allen also Elizabeth Allen, his wife on the next day
November 5th 1811, the 65 year of her age. Father and Mother of
Robert Allen (who records this last tribute to their memory,).

Departed this life March 4, 1794 James Allen, brother of Robert Allen.

Departed this life Oct. 22, 1812, Joseph W. Allen (Brother of Robert Allen).

Departed this life Eliza Allen (daughter of R. Allen) on the 18th day of
February 1816.
  "We mourn thy death, lovely Daughter, for thou wert Dear,
   But why so selfish as to wish you here,
   Where we the ills of Troubled life Indure,
   There, thou art safe to know these ills no more."

DEATHS

Departed this life Sept. 27, 1817 George C. Allen (Brother of Robert Allen)
  at Baton Rouge, La.

Died on Friday evening on the 29 March 1822 in the 34 year of her age,
  Rebecca Allen, wife of Robert Allen, who is left to mourn the loss
  of an angel companion.

Died on Feb. 17th 1827 Margaret McAuley, sister of Robert Allen.

Died at Greenwood on Thursday January the 3d 1828 Caroline W. Allen,
  daughter of Robert Allen in the 17th year of her age.
  "Youth, Innocence and all that was lovely plead, but in vain."

John Allen, brother of Robert Allen departed this life on the 19th day
  of May A.D. 1833 from the kick of a horse in the 57 year of his age.

Dixon T. Allen, died at Gallatin on Friday night 12 oclock, 26 Sept 1834,
where he had gone to attend Court.

Robert Allen Jr. died at New Orleans 5 of February 1836

Died on Tuesday night 10 oclock, July 28, 1840, William Rosin Allen
aged 7 years and four months at Greenwood.

Died on Saturday night about 2 oclock, Aug. 1, 1840 Eliza Clarissa Allen
aged not quite one year. Thus in less than one week, have the parents
been bereft of two lovely children.

Departed this life at Greenwood on Monday evening Aug. 19, A.M. 1844
Robert Allen aged 66 years and 2 months.

James G. Allen
Departed this life in Lafouch, La. April 21, 1855.

David Burford Allen died at Brownsville, Texas, Sept. 7, 1855.

Alethia Allen wife of Robert Allen died Oct. 24, 1862, at Greenwood,
    aged 58 years and 10 days.

Alethia Beal Allen, daughter of Robert and Alethia Allen, died at
    Dr. Lapsleys in Nashville July 6, 1854, aged 19 years 1 mo. and 3 days.

Virginia Dixon Allen Bridges daughter of Robert and Alethia Van Horn Allen
    and wife of Thomas P. Bridges, died at her brother Vans near Gallatin
    Saturday 7 oclock A.M. Aug. 13, 1887.

George Campbell died near Saundersville, Sumner County, Tenn. Friday
    Aug. 23, 1889.

Archibald Van Horn Allen died Thursday 2 oclock Sept. 5, 1889.

Hester Maxwell died March 18, 1844.

Louisa Gibbs, Brown, Allen, Campbell died at Jackson, Tennessee, July 25,
    1892.

Rebecca G. Allison, daughter of Robert & Rebecca Allen, died at the home of
    her daughter, Rebecca Porter, Nashville, Tenn., March 2, 1895.

*   *   *   *   *

Children of George *Meade* and Elizabeth Allen-

James - Born March 31, 1774; Died March 4, 1794.
John - Born Feb. 24, 1776; Died May 19, 1833.
Robert - Born June 19, 1778; Died Aug. 19, 1844
William - Born Aug. 3, 1780; Died Oct. 6, 1856
George Campbell, Born Feb. 16, 1783; Died Sept. 27, 1817
Elizabeth, Born July 25, 1785; Died April 1, 1867
Margaret, Born April 22, 1788; Died Feb. 17, 1827
Joseph Webster, Born March 10, 1792; Died Oct. 22, 1812
Mary Webster Born Aug. 22, 1797; Died Jan. 14, 1889
    (She married George A. Lucas, Nov. 4, 1817, Lucas died June 22, 1832.)

*   *   *   *   *

(Robert Allen - Bible Record   p. 5)   ⑦

"Robert Allen was an officer and acted a conspicuous part in the war
of 1812 under Gen.Andrew Jackson, served his District in Congress of
the United States for several Sessions with great credit. He was also
a member of the Convention that formed the present (1834) Constitution
of Tennessee and filled other offices in his County and State with credit.

"Few men were more popular among his constituents or more useful to the
community in which he lived, respected and beloved and none ever sustained
a character more exemplary, so few died more generally lamented."

            -from the Obituary of Robert Allen at time of his death, and
             copied in the family Bible by his son, Joseph W. Allen.

                    *   *   *   *   *

(Robert Allen Record   p. 6)

⑧

"GREENWOOD"

Note: A reminiscence written by Mrs. Eunice Williams Fite (Mrs. Leonard
Fite) of Nashville, Tenn., who as a child was a frequent visitor at
Greenwood, the home of Robert Allen, near Carthage, Tenn.
Mrs. Fite's mother was Lucy Anne Williams, an intimate friend of
Virginia Allen.

"Since 'Garden Fever' has manifested itself throughout the country
it is meet that a word should be said of old gardens that flourished
several decades ago and live now only in the memory of a few. So I am
making a 'memory pilgrimage' to Greenwood, near Carthage, the lovely old
ante bellum home of Robert Allen built for his distinguished bride,
Rebecca Greer.

"The young mistress of the house followed the traditional idea, rare
personal charm and dignity were hers, as were the virtues exemplifying
the spiritual forces of her day. Those who are familiar with Carthage,
in Smith County, Tennessee, and its environs know that it rivals in
beauty the scenery of the most favored upland countries - the steep bluff,
the winding river, the purple hills are a never-ending delight.

"About a mile and a half northwest of town up the Old Battery hill and
through a wooded drive, flanked on either side by beautiful hills, one
came upon Greenwood. The spot seemed designed by nature for a home.
The house was a two story red brick with white shutters and keystones
over the windows. A brick walk led to a flag-stone terrace and the
hospitable door of the manor. There were no columns.

"On the garden side of the house the earth sloped gently down to a meadow.
On this slope English daisies, pink, white and lavender, carpeted the
ground. The garden was part of the meadow. I recall no geometrical
designs. Grass grew in the center and was bordered by a profusion of
flowers. Lilacs, syringa, snowballs, lemon lillies, roses, peonies, iris,
etc., also the usual herbs that make fragrant the linen shelves and
savoury the cuisine. It was a garden that delighted bees and butterflies
as well as children. At the rear was a latticed summer house which
sheltered the cistern over which trailed a handsome wisteria. The usual
smoke-house and cabins completed the ensemble.

"When a little girl I began accompanying my mother on visits to Greenwood,
Miss Virginia Allen, a daughter of the house being the adored friend of
my mother, a friendship hallowed by the vicissitudes of the Civil War.

Well I remember the last visit, and a sad one, to Greenwood - Miss Virginia,
my mother and I (by then a grown-up young lady) went out to spend the night.
A tenant was in charge - all the loved ones were gone. As we walked up
the brick path to the house, not a word was said, the tears were coursing
down the beautiful face of Miss Virginia Allen, and I, on the threshhold of
life, wondered if it is ever wise to open the door on so many endearing
memories."

                                        Eunice Williams Fite.

Ancestry of Rebecca Greer, wife of Robert Allen.

Special Inscription in Bible (written June 30, 1889, by
Joseph Webster Allen, son of Robert Allen, Sr. and Rebecca Greer.)
Samuel Greer born in Limerick, Ireland, Married Rebecca McCracken
(Grandparents of Jos. W. Allen and Rebecca Allen Allison.)

Samuel & Rebecca Greer, Samuel was born in Ireland 1750, Died in
Jonesboro, Tennessee, 1833 (aged 83 years). Rebecca Greer died near
Jonesboro March 25, 1828, aged 68. They had 3 sons and 5 daughters,
all born at Carlisle, Pennsylvania. They came to Jonesboro in 1790.
Their children were named John, Samuel, Thomas, Catherine, Mary,
Hester, Margaret and Rebecca. Mary was the oldest and was the last one
to die. She married John Chester and died April 5, 1860.
Catherine married John Kennedy, died March 26, 1840.
Hester married a Mr. Kelsey first, then Samuel Maxwell.
Margaret married Isaac B. McClellan.
Rebecca married Robert Allen. She was born Aug. 22, 1787, married
Dec. 25, 1803 in Jonesboro, died near Carthage, Smith County, Tenn.,
March 29, 1822.
Samuel married _____.
John & Thomas neither married.
John lived to be nearly 80.
Mary was born March 1795, married in Jonesboro July 14, 1816,
Died in Somerville, W. Tennessee, June 30, 1889.

*   *   *   *   *

ALLEN

Records from the Bible of John Allen, of Summer County, Tennessee,
Printed and Published by Matthew Carey, 1809, 122 Market St.,
Philadelphia. In the possession of Mrs. Wm. Guild, West End Ave.,
Nashville, Tennessee, daughter of Benjamin F. Allen mentioned herein.
Copied June, 1936 by Miss Matilda Porter.

MARRIAGES

John Allen
&
Laetitia Sanders
Friday 23, Dec. 1808

On Thursday evening
Jany. 22, 1829, Eliza H. Allen
Daughter of John & Letitia Allen
to Sam'l Houston

On Tuesday evening May 20, 1834,
Martha Ann Allen daughter
of John & Letitia Allen to
J. A. Blackmore.

On Thursday evening June 26, 1834,
George W. Allen Son of John & Letitia
Allen to Louisa F. Douglas.

August 1837 James Sanders Allen
son of John and Leititia Allen to
Mary Moss.

November the 8, 1840
Eliza H. Houston to
Elmore Douglas.

Joseph Campbell Allen
to Susan O. Trousdale
Oct. 27, 1847.

Benjamin F. Allen and
Louisa Trousdale were married
January 31st 1850

Martha A. Douglas to Dr. W. D. Haggard
July 5, 1859.

(John Allen - Bible Records   p. 2)

BIRTHS

of John & Laetitia Allen and their
family.

John Allen was born Feb. 24, 1776

Laetitia, wife of John Allen was born Feb. 27
1792

Eliza H. Allen daughter of John & Laetitia
Allen was born Saturday night Dec. 2 1809

George Webster Allen son of John & Laetitia
Allen was born Sunday night Dec. 8, 1811.

Martha Ann Allen was born Thursday night
Feby 2nd 1814

Hariet Allen was born Wednesday
morning May the 1st 1816

James Sanders Allen son of John &
Laetitia Allen was born Wednesday
morning Sept. 15, 1819

Joseph Campbell Allen son of John &
Laetitia Allen was Born Friday
morning Jany 9th 1824.

Benjamin Franklin Allen son of John &
Laetitia Allen was Born Monday night
the 6th of March 1826

Charles Granderson Allen, son of John &
Letitia Allen was born Tuesday night
May 6, 1829.

Margaret M. Allen, Daughter of John & Letitia
Allen was born Tuesday night, May 16, 1830

Letitia Sanders Allen daughter of John &
Letitia Allen was born Thursday morning
Nov. 22, 1832.

Martha Allen Douglas daughter of
Elmore and Eliza Douglas was born
Sept. the 11, 1841.

Mary Trousdale daughter of J. C. &
Susan O. Allen Friday evening
born August 4th 1848

(John Allen - Bible Records p. 3)

Births Continued

Hariet Louisa daughter of Elmore &
Eliza Douglas, born Sept. 2nd
1843

William Howard son of Elmore
& Eliza Douglas, born 29th June
1848

Susan Miller Douglass daughter of Elmore
and Eliza Douglas was born Nov. 28th
1853

Louisa Douglas Haggard first
born of Wm. D. and Martha A. Haggard was
born May 3, 1860.

DEATHS

Departed this life Nov. 4th 1811
George Allen, Father of John Allen
in the 61 year of his age

Departed this life Nov. 5, 1811
Elizabeth Allen Mother of Jno. Allen
in the 65 year of her age.

Departed this life March 2 1794 James
Allen son of George & Elizabeth Allen
and Brother to John Allen in the 20
year of his age.

Departed this life Oct. 22d 1812 Joseph
W. Allen son of Geo. & Elizabeth Allen
& Bro. to John Allen in the 20 year of his age

Departed this life at Baton Rouge Louisiana
on Saturday Sept. 27, 1817 George Campbell
Allen son of George & Elizabeth Allen
and Brother of John Allen in the
34 year of his age.

Eliza H. Douglas daughter of John &
Letitia Allen & Consort of Dr. Elmore
Douglas departed this life after a
long and painful illness on Sabath
Eve March 3, 1861 aged 51 years
3 months & 1 day.

13

Deaths Continued

Departed this life on Saturday night
the 17th of Feb. 1827 half past 9 oclock
Peggy McCauly, daughter of George and
Elizabeth Allen and sister of John
Allen in the 38th year of her age.

Departed this life on Wednesday
night March 18, 1829, Charles Grandison
Allen son of John & Letitia Allen
Aged Ten Months & twelve days.

Departed this life on Thursday Morning
20 minutes past 9 oclock, Nov. 29, 1832
Letitia Allen wife of John Allen
in the 40 year of her age leaving
an infant daughter of 8 days old.

Departed this life Sunday evening
3 oclock May 19, 1833 John Allen
in the 68 year of his age.

Margaret M. Allen departed this life
Friday April 17, 1863.

Departed this life on Friday evening
15 minutes after 3 oclock, May 31 1839,
Letitia Sanders Allen youngest
daughter of John & Letitia Allen in
the Seventh year of her age.

Died Thursday Morning 9 oclock, Feb. 25th
1850, William Howard son of Elmore
and Eliza H. Douglas aged 19 months.

Departed this life Jany. 23, 1853, John C. Allen
in the 29th year of his age, also his Son
John C. Allen 21st Feby following, between 3
& 4 years old.

Susan M. Douglass daughter of Elmore and
Eliza H. Douglass died Sunday January
the 19th 1879 at 4 1/2 oclock P.M.

George Webster Allen died Saturday
May 25th 1881 at 6 1/2 oclock A.M.

James Sanders Allen died Sunday
June 24 1894 at 3 oclock.

B. F. Allen died March 10, 1910.

SMITH COUNTY

COLBERT BIBLE

This Bible was originally owned by Archibald J. Colbert, of Smith County.
It is now owned by Mrs. G. U. Thompson, Carthage, Tennessee, Rt. #2.

BIRTHS
Archibald J. Colbert born Jan. 6, 1830
Mary B.   "   "   May 29, 1831
James Wesley   "   "   Oct. 25, 1853
Susan B. Colbert   "   Feb. 3, 1855
Leonard   "   "   Feb. 22, 1859
William King Stallings "   Oct. 22, 1858

DEATHS
Susan M. Timb died Aug. 20, 1853
Mary B. Colbert died June 4, 1859

MARRIAGES
Archibald J. Colbert and Mary B. Timb
Married 18 Nov. 1852.

*   *   *

HALE BIBLE RECORD

Taken from the Bible of William Hale, now owned by Odell Haile, Hunter's Point Road (West of Payne's Store), Trousdale County, Tennessee. Copied by Mrs. Rhea E. Garrett, July, 1936.

William Hale & Prissey Cage were married April 25, 1787.

William Haile was born February 2nd, 1759
Priscilla Cage was born September 22nd, 1768

Cage Haile was born April the 19th, 1788
Elizabeth Haile was born August the 12th, 1789
Sarah Hale was born March the 10th, 1791
Nicholas Hale was born June the 10th 1792
Wilson Hale was born June the 10th, 1792
William Hale was born June the 4th 1794
Richard Hale was born August the 12th 1795
James Hale was born October the 11th 1796
Edward D. Hale was born November the 8th 1797
Prissay Hale was born July the 2nd 1799
Jessey Hale was born September the 20, 1801
John B. Hale was born September the 23, 1804
Cyrus B. Hale was born November the 22, 1807
Eliza T. Taylor was born September the 1st 1810

MARRIAGES

Joseph Young and Elizabeth Hale were married March the 9th 1809

Robert M. Moores and Sarah Hale were married April 1809
Cage Haile and Rebeccka Rankin were married November the 2nd 1809

Wilson Hale and Nancy Ann H. Crutcher were married September the 24th 1818

Richard Hale and Mary J. Young was mared March the 15 inst 1819

Edward D. Hale & Prissilla Hale was married December the 18th 1825

*   *   *

(16)

SMITH COUNTY

HALE FAMILY BIBLE

Children of Nicholas and Sarah Hale:

BIRTHS

Rachel Amanda Haile was bornd May the 26th   1822
Elizabeth Malvina Hale was bornd October the 11th   1824
William C. Hale was bornd July the 28th 1826
Elizabeth M. Moore was born the 22nd October 1810
Prissella Almira Hale daughter of N. and Sarah Hale was born March the 19th
    182(8)?
Elizar Young was born the 25 of february 1815-
Eliza Young was b. -   -   -   -

    Herbert Lipscomb was born Oct. 15, 1875
    Nannie Elizabeth Lipscomb was born June the 24th   1880

Edward M. Haile was born May the 29th   1806

Priscilla Ann Hale was born September the 18th   1834
William Joseph Hale was born the 10th March   1836
James Cage Hale was born June 30th 1846
Louellar Hale was born August th 15th   1853.
Samuel J. Harper and Priscilla Ann Hale was married the 11th   1854.

Sarah was born September   1833

Martha Ann, the daughter of Sarah and Bobs or Boles was born November the 28,
    1851.
Nancy L. Jane was born Oct. the 15th this 1859.
Rubin Cage was born June the 23th A.D. 1855.
Burton was born August the 24 A.D. 1856
Susan Malisey was bornd Febry the 4th   1860
Mary Wiley was born May th 28   1861

Samuel J. Harper was born March 20, 1832.
James William Harper was Born August the 11th   1856,
And Departed His Life on the 6th Oct. 1856
Bennetta Harper was bornd Augus the 15the   1857.
Nancy Elizabeth Harper was bornd June the 20the   1860
D. C. Harper was born October the 5th   1866
Marietta Harper was born March the 5th   18___2 (?)

DEATHS

Elizabeth Young died Nov. the 5th   1821

(Smith County - Hale Family Bible p. 2)

DEATHS (Cont'd.)

William Hale Senr. Departed this life June the 29th 1822
James Hale Deceased this life 1833, June 6th.
Priscilla Hale Deceased this life September the 6th 1849.
P. A. Harper Consort of D. J. Harper Died April 20th 1867.
E. P. Hale Died October the 29th 1886
Cyrus B. Hale Died March 17, 1887.

                    *   *   *

SMITH COUNTY

BIBLE RECORD
JAMES BARTLEY HUBBARD FAMILY BIBLE

This is a large bible, about 75 years old, owned by Mrs. James Bartley Hubbard, Brush Creek, Tennessee.
Copied by Mrs. Bessie Gibbs, Carthage, Tennessee.
July 27, 1937.

MARRIAGES

This is to certify that J. B. Hubbard and J. C. Ligon were united by me in Holy Matrimony at J. A. Ligon's on the 11th day of November in the year of our Lord 1880, in presence of many friends & relatives. Signed, J. P. Carter, J. P.

J. R. Gibbs & Carie P. Hubbard was united in marriage October 16th. 1902.

J. C. Hubbard & Ida W. Waggoner was united in marriage November 7, 1915.

C. W. Hubbard & Beaulah M. Gibbs was united in marriage December 25, 1919.

O. J. Hubbard & Nannie B. Carter was united in marriage December 25, 1928.

B. M. Hubbard & Elizabeth Jones were united in marriage December 25, 1930.

BIRTHS

Beaulah Gibbs Hubbard was born July 1, 1897
J. C. Ligon was born January 17, 1859
Carrie P. Hubbard was born A. D. September 24, 1881
Cleveland W. Hubbard was born A. D. August 18th. 1885
Benton M. Hubbard was born A. D. May 30th. 1888
James C. Hubbard was born A . D. September 4, 1891
Ottis J. Hubbard was born A. D. January 6th. 1900
J. B. Hubbard was born September 20, 1856

DEATHS

Carrie P. Gibbs Departed this life A. D. 1916, November 26th.
James B. Hubbard Departed this life A. D. 1930, October 2.

SMITH COUNTY

BIBLE RECORD
THOS. P. LIGON FAMILY BIBLE

This Bible is very old, backs are torn off and gone and unable to tell when printed. First owned by Thos. P. Ligon, present owner Mrs. Ella Ligon Stallings, Brush Creek, Tennessee.
Copied by Mrs. Bessie Gibbs, Carthage, Tennessee.
July 27, 1937.

MARRIAGES

Joan Ligon was married to Isaac Boulton 2nd. November 1864

Lurana Jane Ligon was mared to Jonithan Clark on the 15 of October 1868

Drusille J. Ligon was married to Harrison L. Duglis (Douglass?)
                              September 26, 1869

James W. Ligon was married to Eliza Hubbard October 11, 1869

Margie M. Ligon's marriage to Wm. T. Tyree November 23, 1876

Fannie C. Ligon was married to J. P. Sanders October 7th. 1874

Alfred P. Ligon Married to Sallie Tyree November 18th. 1885

Marriage of D. R. Lester and E. C. Ligon November 30th. 1881

Marriage of W. R. Stallings and Ella Ligon November 19, 1885

George S. Ligon was married to Mandy J. Stallings October 23rd. 1887

Geo. S. Ligon & Malvinia Ballinger were married June 1895

Geo. S. Ligon & Melissa Smartt were married November 8, 1914

DEATHS

Minnie B. Ligon, daughter of A. B. & Sallie Ligon was born September
the 10th. 1866 and died February the 7, 1893
Lillie Ligon Thaxton died February 29, 1920
Thos. P. Ligon died February 11, 1900
Mary Bains Ligon died June 1909
Geo. S. Ligon died November --
Sallie Ligon died - - -
Malvina Ligon died May 1912
Benton Ligon died 1920 (?)
Alice Ligon died 1870
May Sussan Douglass died ---

(Thos. P. Ligon Family Bible, p. 2)

BIRTHS

Thos. P. Ligon was born October 23, 1820
Drusilla Sampson Ligon was born June 24, 1815
Mary Hammock Bains Ligon died (born) March 29, 1826

DEATHS

Thos. P. Ligon died February 11, 1900
Drusilla Sampson Ligon died September 28, 1858
Mary Hammock Bains Ligon died June 27, 1909

MARRIAGES

Thos. P. Ligon & Drusilla Sampson were married November 11, 1841

Thos. P. Ligon & Mary Hammock Bains were married January 16, 1861

DEATHS

Drusilla Ligon Douglass died October 25, 1876
Fannie C. Ligon Sanders died July 15, 1886
William B. Ligon died September 4, 1894

BIRTHS

Lurana Jane Ligon born September 19, 1842
Joan White Ligon born May 15, 1844
James Watt Ligon born May 4, 1846
Thos, Jefferson Ligon born July 30, 1848
Mary Matilda Ligon May 3, 1850
Drusilla Ligon April 14, 1852
Frances Ligon January 8, 1808
Alfred B. Ligon May 18, 1862
George Samuel Ligon October 23, 1867
Emily Christiana Ligon November 15, 1863
Elizabeth Ella Ligon September 1, 1865
William B. Ligon April 18, 1870

SMITH COUNTY

BIBLE RECORD
WM. W. LIGON FAMILY BIBLE

This Bible is very old, torn apart and part gone - is owned by a granddaughter, Mrs. Capitola Hubbard, Brush Creek, Tennessee. Mrs. Hubbard is now 78 years old.
Copied by Mrs. Bessie Gibbs, Carthage, Tennessee.
July 26, 1937.

BIRTHS

William W. Ligon was born December 14th. 1783
Jane Ligon was born February 15, 1796

MARRIAGES

Wm. W. Ligon & Jane Ligon was married, November 2d. 1809

BIRTHS

John C. Ligon was bornd November 8, 1810
W. C. Ligon was bornd November 6, 1812
James C. Ligon was bornd August 4, 1814
M. L. Ligon was bornd April 22, 1817
G. W. Ligon was bornd November 18, 1818
Thos. P. Ligon was bornd October 23, 1820
Thimothy W. Ligon was bornd November 18, 1822

DEATHS

G. W. Ligon Dec'd. September 3, 1840
W. W. Ligon Dec'd. March 11th. 1823
Jane Ligon Departed this life February 15th. 1865 - age 69-11-7

SMITH COUNTY

BIBLE RECORD
HEZEKIAH STALLINGS FAMILY BIBLE

This Bible is real old, torn apart and am unable to tell how old it is. The first owner Hezekiah Stallings, second H. H. Stallings, present owner Wm. Richard Stallings, Brush Creek, Tennessee. Mr. Wm. Richard Stallings is now 77 years old.
Copied by Mrs. Bessie Gibbs, Carthage, Tennessee.
July 27, 1937

BIRTHS

Elizabeth Carter, daughter of John S. Carter and Ann his wife, was born on the 27th. of May 1825
Hezekiah H. Stallings, son of John Stallings & Katherine his wife, was born the 6 day of February 1816
Letter Ann Stallings, daughter of Hezekiah Stallings & Elizabeth his wife, was born the 4th. of April 1843
Catherine Patience Stallings, daughter of Hezekiah Stallings and Elizabeth his wife, was born the 12th. of August 1845
John Stowers Stallings, son of H. H. Stallings & Elizabeth his wife, was born the 19th. of May 1851
Thos. Hale Stallings, son of H. H. Stallings & Elizabeth his wife, was born the 2nd. of October 1853
Wm. Richard Stallings, son of H. H. Stallings & Elizabeth his wife, was born the 21st. of November 1860
Amanda Jane Stallings, daughter of H. H. Stallings & Elizabeth his wife, was born April 2nd. 1866
Ella E. Ligon was born September 1st. 1865
Wm. Geo. Stallings was born November 22, 1886
Mary Elizabeth Stallings was born September 13, 1888
Lassie Christiana Stallings was born October 7th. 1889
Thos. Hezekiah Stallings was born June 22nd. 1892
Joe Stallings was born July 1st. 1895
Charlie John Stallings was born April 9, 1901
Ralph Dewitt Stallings was born September 2nd. 1904

MARRIAGES

W. R. Stallings was married to Ella Ligon November 19, 1885

W. G. Stallings was married to Ollie P. Harel January 12, 1913

Joe P. Pendleton was married to Lassye Stallings October 18, 1914

Joe Stallings was married to Etta House September 1919

Ralph D. Stallings and Bessie Lynch were married February 28, 1926

(Hezekiah Stallings Family Bible, p. 2)

DEATHS

Mary Elizabeth Stallings died November 17, 1888
Thos. H. Stallings died in Commercy, France January 28, 1919 (died of
bronchial pneumonia, a soldier in Worlds War)
Charlie John Stallings died April 14, 1929 at Colfax, Calif. of T. B.

TOMBSTONE - INSCRIPTIONS

BILL ALLMON GRAVEYARD
SMITH COUNTY

Graveyard is located about 100 yards on right of Highway, 2
miles from Gordonsville, Tennessee, on road leading to New
Middleton, Tennessee. From Carthage, Tenn., cross Cordell
Hull Bridge across Cumberland River, turn left, keep this
road about $\frac{3}{4}$ mile, turn right on New Middleton Road 2 miles,
graveyard 100 yards on right on what is known as Whitley Hill.
    Land first owned by Fannie McDonald Allmon, 2nd, Lee
Whitley,(col),now owned by Marvin Lyles (col.).
There are about 50 unmarked graves. (Bill Allmon and wife,
Fannie McDonald Allmon, and daughters,Para Lee Allmon Hunt,
Maggie Allmon Stewart; grand-daughter Holland Hunt Ballard,
are buried here, but no markers.(Information obtained by copy-
ist from Mrs. Sopha McDonald Agee, Gordonsville, Tennessee,
Star Route.)
Copied by Mrs. Bessie Gibbs, Carthage, Tennessee.
May 31, 1937.

MCDONALD:
Sterling Brown,
Aug. 23, 1846.
Aug. 22, 1910.
Co. G. M.T.D. Inf. 4 Tenn.

Martha Frances,
Apr. 7, 1851.
May 9, 1933.

TOMBSTONE - INSCRIPTIONS

CARTER GRAVEYARD
SMITH COUNTY

Located about 4 miles from Carthage, Tennessee, on the Tilmon-Dixon Highway, # 24, Lebanon Pike. Turn to right at first side road, about 3 miles, it is about 1 mile from this point. Copied by Mrs. Bessie Gibbs and Miss Hattie Winfree, Carthage, Tennessee. There are about 50 graves with rocks-no inscriptions. March 31, 1937.

Willie West Uhles,
July 30, 1878.

W. B. Uhles,
Born & Died Nov. 8, 1894.

M. B. Uhles,
Aug. 1896.

G. B. Uhles,
Jan. 25, 1905.
Aug. 22, 1906.

G. W. Uhles,
Sept. 3, 1910.

W. C. West,
July 19, 1847.
Died ---?

Amanda Eugenia West,
Jan. 12, 1841.
Oct. 22, 1911.

John S. West,
Mar. 24, 1866.
Aug. 18, 1897.

Celia Waggoner, Wife of
Jacob Waggoner,
Born May 7, 1808.
Joines Hogan's Creek
Baptist Church,
Sept. 24, 1834.
Died Oct. 23, 1878.
" I am dying, thank God,
Thank God."

Thomas A. Waggoner,
Born Aug. 16, 1834.
Died June 10, 1876.

Elizabeth Waggoner, Wife of
Thomas A. Waggoner,
Born July, 1834.
Died Feb. 10, 1872.

Nancy, G. Waggoner,
July 11, 1859.
Oct. 20, 1934.

Jacob H. Waggoner,
May 29, 1852.
Dec. 24, 1892.
(This Jacob H. Waggoner
was the husband of Nancy G.
Waggoner, and son of Celia
& Jacob Waggoner.)

Mary S. Carter,
July 22, 1841.
Died Oct. 1913.

(Masonic Emblem)
John P. Carter,
Born Jan. 30, 1828.
Died Apr. 21, 1904.

Annie Whitley, Wife of
W. B. Whitley,
Born Sept. 12, 1819.
Died June 11, 1849.

W. D. Hensley,
Aug. 8, 1914-Dec. 17, 1917.
"Budded on earth, to bloom
in heaven."

This page was very faint in the original.

SMITH COUNTY

TOMBSTONE RECORDS

SECOND CARTHAGE CEMETERY

This cemetery is located west of Carthage about one hundred yards from the square. This was formerly a Methodist Church Graveyard. The church has been torn down and a new one built on Main Street. The lot left has been included in the Cemetery. There are a few small stones in this graveyard unmarked. Copied by Geraldine Smith September 2, 1936. There is another oldergraveyard adjoining this one, on the North side.

Eliza J. wife of W.B. Pickering born Apr 22, 1843 died Jan. 28,1888
William B. Pickering Mar. 21,1844 died May 21, 1919
Henrietta H. Pickering Feb. 14, 1856-Dec 8, 1926.

Melissa Fisher Oliver Jan. 12, 1854 Feb. 18,1928
Horace B. Oliver Apr 6, 1848 May 12,1917

John A. Fite Born Feb. 10, 1832 died Aug. 23, 1925
Col 7th Tenn Inf C.S.A. Lawyer Soldier Jurist
Mary M. Mitchell wife of John A. Fite Born Aug. 21, 1846 died Aug. 18,1890

R. D. Flippen Born March 1, 1827 Died Jan 18,1891
Tennessee Flippen Born Apr. 23, 1831 died Aug 27,1873

A. E. Garrett Mar. 6, 1830 Feb 14, 1907
Louisa wife of Col. A.E.Garrett Born Aug 22, 1835 died June 19,1877
Augusta E. Garrett wife of A.J.Redditt Born Feb. 28,1853 died Dec 17,1878
Sarah Flowers Garrett wife of Stephen Garrett & mother of Col. A.E.Garrett
                           born June 8, 1808 Jan. 4,1881
C.W.Garrett Atty at Law June 20, 1858 July 16, 1904

J.H.Smith Born July 25,1823 Jan 14,1900
Harriet J. Smith Born May 16,1826 Died July 25,1912
A.J. Redditt Oct. 1, 1847 Mar 3, 1918
his wife Eliza J. Dec. 6, 1858 June 15, 1922

Betty Ward 1859-1917

Welcome Martin Savage July 21,1838 July 22, 1912

Joseph Samuel Wilson Born Nov. 14,1838 Died July 3, 1885
Kitty D. Wilson Born Mar. 24, 1815 Died June 29, 1892

E.W.Turner Born July 7, 1832 Died May 22, 1902

Sallie M. Hart Born July 30, 1854 Died June 2, 1918
Henry Eugene Hart B. May 4, 1852 D July 22, 1899

Mary J. wife of Capt S. B. McDearman born Aug. 3, 1831 Died May 5, 1878

Helen Strother Lee wife of Joseph Myer July 22, 1842 Oct. 11,1913 (27)

Joseph Myer Aug 15, 1883 Mar 9, 1899

P. G. Dillard Born Feb. 14, 1835 Died Oct 9, 1893

Horace M. Hale Mar 23, 1844 July 1, 1924
Cornelia Wilson wife of H.M.Hale Mar. 19,1844 Dec. 22, 1904

Nancy N. Jordan Born Apr 13, 1824 Died June 4, 1901
Samantha D. wife of John B. Jordan Born Oct. 17, 1846 Died Aug 26, 1883

Gertrude wife of W.W.Ford B. March 8, 1853 Died Dec 31, 1889

Sarah Agness infant daughter of A.G. & M.M. Pickering death July 8,1847
aged 4 months

Wirt Vaden Lee 1856-1927

James Monroe Fisher Feb. 12, 1844 Apr 1, 1909

Robert McGee King 1847-1884

W.D. Gold May 23, 1848 Aug 17, 1911

Catherine M. Goodpasture Born Sept. 8, 1830 Died Aug. 20, 1898

Melissa wife of Dr. R.L.Duval Jan. 8, 1856 Oct 1, 1921

Mrs. Mary A. Sanders Born June 1, 1849 Died June 29, 1903

John Lewis Goodall Born June 15, 1815 Died Aug. 21, 1858

Bethenia B. Crutcher wife of A.A. Swope Born July 9, 1825
Died Oct. 24, 1882
Archibald A. Swope Born Dec 26, 1819 Died Oct 25, 1894

Rebecca N. wife of Jno. Sneed Born Dec 31, 1818 Died Oct 6, 1881

Charles W. Smith Died June 12, 1889 aged about 59 years.

John V. Turner Sec. Son of E. P. & Mary E. Turner: Born Dec. 21, 1852
Died Jan. 30, 1859

F. L. G. Inf. Dau. of F. P. & Mary E. Turner; Died Sept. 8, 1858
Aged 3 yrs & 1 mo. & 21 Days.

Belle McClarin Born 1832-Died Apr. 3, 1902.

Mary J. Consort of H. W. McClarin Died Aug. 19, 1854; Aged 18 yrs.

Hugh & Mary McClarin Natives of Tyrone, Ireland; Died Nov. 24, 1872.
She Died Feb. 28, 1864.

James McClarin B. 1825-Died 1904. Jennie Wife Born 1836-1896.

William G. Son of T. P. Hr. & Jessie Brides Born Aug. 6, 1897
Died Aug. 14, 1897.

Callie Daughter of George W. & Fanney Lynch Born Oct. 17, 1878
Died July 17, 188-. (?)
(Date not given)

Mary J. Fisher Wife of T. F. Born Apr. 24, 1822; Died Apr. 29, 1885.

Thomas Fisher Born Apr. 24, 1817, Died Sept. 8, 1880.

Amanda E. Daughter of T. & J. F. Born Apr. 22, 1847; Died Dec. 24, 1863

Abram K. Son of T. & J. F. Born Dec. 28, 1856; Died May 5, 1869.

Martin H. Daughter of F. & J. Fisher Bn. Aug. 7, 1851½ Died May 11,1869

Willie DeWitt Died Nob. 26, 1863; Aged 1 yr. 5½mo.
Emilia Price wife of Wm Henry DeWitt Died Nov. 26, 1863;Aged 4 days
Alonzo DeWitt Died Nov. 27, 1863; Aged 15 yrs.

Mandy M. Wife of Wm. Bryant Born Nov. 12, 1862; Died Dec. 21, 1899

G. K. C. Salter Born Aug. 10, 1870; Died Nov. 1, 1895.

Annie C. Daughter of D. N. & Mattie McDonald Born Dec. 15, 1899
Died Nov. 11, 1900

Julia G. Daughter of Relict of N. B. McDonald Born Feb. 18, 1817
Died Aug. 31, 1902.

Col. H. B. McDonald Born Feb 27, 1794; Died May 22, 1873.

Clara David Daughter of David M. & Clara McDonald; Born Aor.28, 1889
Died July 4, 1889

D. N. McDonald Born Oct. 10, 1866 Died Jan 10, 1902.

H   Hettie Rose Goodpasture wife of B. F. Sanders; Apr. 21, 1871
                                                June 6, 1906.
     Catherine M. Goodpasture, Born Sept. 8, 1830; Died Aug. 20, 1898.

     Dr. R. L. Duval Died Jan 1.1, 1935; Aged 76 yr, 8 mos & 23 days.

     Melissa Wife of Dr. R. L. Duval Jan. 8, 1856; Oct. 1, 1821.

     Elizabeth March 17, 1918; Died July 14, 1919.

     Rebecca N. Wife of John Sneed; Born Dec. 31, 1818; Died Oct. 26, 1881

     Archibald A. Swope Born Dec. 26, 1819 Died Oct. 25, 1894.

     Louisa Rebecca Daughter of David & Nancy Hogg; Born Apr. 24, 1821
Married D. J. S. Cornwell   Died Nov. 15, 1890

     Dr. John S. Cornwell Born Pittsylvania County, Va, Mar. 14, 1816.
                Died--.

     Major Jas. M. Scantland; Born in Caroline Co., Va. Sept. 4, 1796
                    Died July 22, 1849.

     Campbell Burke, Son of Louisa G. Pickett Died Sept. 9, 1849.

     Oscar F. Howard Born Nov. 20, 1812, Died Mar. 23, 1847.

     Leroy E. Mitchell Born Aug. 26, 1811; Died Aug. 5, 1863.

BettieBettie W. Mitchell Born Mar. 23, 1844; Died Nov. 29, 1863.

     Elizabeth Watkins Howard Born Dec. 26, 1816; Married to L. E.
Mitchell Nov. 1, 1836.   Died Apr. 30, 1846.

     Samuel P. Howard Born in Lancaster Co., Va. Feb. 20, 1790
                    Died Dec. 19, 1857.

     Lucy B. Cunningham Wife of S. P. Howard Died Feb. 7, 1869
                              Aged 77 yrs.

     Lucy B. Mitchell Born Nov. 27, 1837; Died July 4, 1858.

     Luvenia E. Daughter of P. F. & Elizabeth Cornwell; Born Nov. 6, 1849
                                          Died May 7, 1852.

     Col. Pleasant F. Cornwell Born in Pittsa Co., Va. Dec. 16, 1813
Shot by David B. Allen, Age 40 yrs, 4 mos. 11 days.   Jan. 27, 1854.

     Little Nellie Died July 4, 1877; Aged 6 yrs; 1 mo. & 7D

     James P. McKee Born Jan. 12, 1815; Died Apr. 12, 1881

     Charles W. Smith Died June 12, 1889; Aged about 59 yrs.

     R. C. Williams Nov. 29, 1862; Apr. 12, 1896.

CARTHAGE, CEMETERY (CONTINUED)

Jas. Berry Moores (Lawyer); Nov. 3, 1807; Died May 23, 1869
Mrs. J. B. Luster only child.

Elizabeth B. Moores consort of Jas. B. Moores born Oct. 14, 1812
                                                Died Nov. 11, 1861.

Infant Son of M. J. & N. H. Malone born Aug. 6, 1895; Died Mar. 31, 1896

Inf. of S. R. & Drucilla Malone born & Died Dec. 22, 1901

Nannie H. Violet wife of M. J. Malone Born Apr. 29, 1857;
                                                Died Oct., 2, 1921.

Rhoda Violet Malone Died Mar. 8, 1936; Aged 46 yrs.
(This is not a tombstone but a marker.)

John Halsell Gardenhire born 1845; Died 1920.

Eliza Snodgrass Gardenhire 1853-1912.

Fannie Boulton Born Oct. 20, 1858; Died Apr. 6, 1893.

There are 51 graves in this cemetery with rough stones.

TOMBSTONE - INSCRIPTIONS

CHESTNUT MOUND GRAVEYARD
SMITH COUNTY

Located about ten miles East of Carthage, Tennessee, on the
South Side of U.S. Highway # 70, behind the Methodist Church.
This graveyard is well kept.
There are 68 unmarked graves.
Copied by Mrs. Cora Whitefield, Carthage, Tennessee.
March 29, 1937.

Gradie Fitzpatrick,
Born Mar. 4, 1896.
Died Sept. 2, 1896.
" Budded on earth,
To bloom in heaven."

Sam S. Fitzpatrick,
Died Jan. 25, 1936.
Born-----?
Aged ----?

(Glover Marker)
FATHER:
E. B. Glover,
Born July 15, 1878.
Died June 6, 1928.
" Thy God has claimed
thee as his own."
MOTHER:
Pearl Glover,
Born Feb. 25, 1893.
Died ----,?
" There is rest in heaven."

J. Y. Ditty,
Feb. 5, 1872.
July 4, 1936.

DITTY:
Cora, Wife of
J. Y. Ditty,
Nov. 29, 1880.
Apr. 15, 1931.
" Rest mother,rest in
quiet sleep, While
friends in sorrow
O'er thee weep."

Rossie P. Petty,
July 24, 1898.
Oct. 19, 1918.
"Darling, We miss thee"

(Petty Marker)
Henry Petty,
Born Nov. 6, 1841.
Died Oct. 27, 1914.
"Thy memory shall ever be
a guiding star to heaven."

Harriet Petty,
Born Sept. 7, 1837.
Died Jan. 23, 1914.
"Faithful to her trust
even unto death."

Mary B. Harris,
Died June 5, 1929.
Age 16 yrs.2 mos.10 da.

To my Wife,Martha,E. wife of
W. B. Traywick.
Died Feb. 7, 1914.
Age about 51 years.
"A loving wife, a mother
dear,lies buried here."

MOTHER:
Mary J. Trawick,
Aug. 12, 1843.
FATHER:
R. B. Trawick,
Nov. 14, 1848.
Dec. 2, 1924.
TRAWICK.

Foutch Marker.
Allie Foutch,
Sept. 21, 1892.
Oct. 17, 1918.

Catherine Foutch, wife of
T. J. Foutch,
March 22, 185--?
Apr. 13, 1936.

Claud Foutch,
Jan. 24, 1894.
Oct. 27, 1896.

Thomas Foutch,
July 15, 1856.
Oct. 28, 1925.

Lizzie Mai, Dau.of
M.A. & C.C. Foutch,
Born Oct. 27, 1907.
Died Nov. 24, 1911.
" How desolate our home,
Bereft of thee."

WEBSTER:
Edgar, Son of
S.S. & Edith Webster,
Apr. 23, 1913.
Oct. 31, 1926.

Henry Ballard,
Oct. 7, 1872.
May 27, 1935.

Bryan Ballard,
Sep. 26, 1901.
May 22, 1925.
" A little time on earth
he spent; Till God for
him his angel sent."

Martha E. Fitzpatrick,
Born Dec. 18, 1839.
Died Sept. 28, 1904.

W. J. Fitzpatrick,
Apr. 27, 1830.
Died Sep. 15, 1901.
" An honest man,the noblest
work of God."

Mollie Petty,
Born May 8, 1866.
Died Oct. 5, 1896.
"Her Spirit smiles from
that bright shore,and softly
whispers,Weep no more."

Robert W. Fitzpatrick,
Apr. 17. 1925.
June 27, 1927.
"Darling, we miss thee."

Peggy Marie Fitzpatrick,
Nov. 9, 1926.
Jan. 25, 1928.
"A sunbeam from the world
has vanished."

Ira B. Cowan,
Apr. 3, 1885.
May 24, 1930.

Virgil Fields,
Aug. 18, 1893.
Dec. 15, 1928.

Bettie Bernice Gunn,
Died Mar. 31, 1935.
Age 1 yr. 11 mos.2 days.

Alline-   Glenn-
June 17,1899.Aug. 17,1901.
Infants of Dr. B. J. and
Ina High.

Cyrus S. Young,
Aug. 11, 1896.
Mar. 20, 1926.
"He is not dead,but sleepeth."

Eunice Roberta Young,
Born June 15, 1918.
Died Oct. 7, 1921.
"Earth has no sorrow that
heaven cannot heal."

Mary Belle Young,
June 8, 1859.
Sept. 18, 1932.
John M. Young,
Oct. 18, 1861.
Aug. 28, 1900.
MOTHER AND FATHER.

(Chestnut Mound Graveyard p.3)

Infant son of
J.T. & M.L. Brown,
Born & Died Jan. 28, 1911.
" Budded on earth to bloom
in heaven."

Sallie B., Wife of
J. H. Warren,
Mar. 18, 1885.
Oct. 30, 1918.
" She faltered by the
wayside, and the angels
took her home."

J. H. Warren,
Mar. 20, 1881.
June 23, 1929.
" May the resurrection
find thee on the
bosom of thy God."

A. J. Calicoat,
Oct. 2, 1850.
Jan. 26, 1933.
" A friend to his Country,
And a believer in Christ."

Lum Swift, (Deaf Mute)
Died Apr. 17, 1926.
Age about 60 yrs.
" An honest man, the
noblest work of God."

Bettie Clariot Cash,
Sept. 9, 1860.
Dec. 3, 1918.
" There is rest in heaven."

Roy Allison, Son of
Mr. & Mrs. R.L. McCaleb,
Dec. 1, 1926.
Nov. 20, 1930.
" Budded on earth to
bloom in heaven."

Infant of H.& M.B.Womack,
Born & Died Nov. 1,1905.
" Budded on earth to
bloom in heaven."

At Rest:
Fred Scudder,
Born Feb. 2, 1885.
Died July 8, 1906.
" Beneath this stone in
soft repose, Is laid a
mother's dearest pride."

Virginia Jared Scudder,
Sept. 4, 1846.
Nov. 12, 1926.
" I know that my Redeemer
liveth."
Wirt Shelby, Son of
J.A.& M.A. Sanders,
July 4, 1910.
Sept. 3, 1916.
"Sleep on dear child,
And take thy rest,
In Jesus arms forever
blest."

Ada A. Apple,
Aug. 8, 1854.
Mar. 17, 1920.
Robert G. Apple,
July 7, 1840.
Mar. 1, 1919.
"God gave, He took, He
will restore; He doeth
all things well."
Mother and Father.

Pearl M. Apple, Wife of
Monsien Cooper,
Born Sep. 16, 1881.
Died Jan. 27, 1907.
"Blessed are the pure in
heart for they shall
see God."

George H. Tumlin,
Apr. 14, 1845.
Oct. 27, 1909.
"Gone but not forgotten."

Robert G. Beasley,
Died Feb. 24, 1934.
Aged 67 years.

Margaret Petty,
Apr. 14, 1869.
Apr. 13, 1927.
" Jesus loves the
pure and holy."

N. J. Petty,
Dec. 19, 1844.
Dec. 25, 1922.
" An honest man, the
Noblest work of God."

Harriet Smith,
Died Oct. 28, 1928.

William Smith,
Died Dec. 31, 1934.
Age about 90 years.
" We will meet again."

TOMBSTONE - INSCRIPTIONS

L.B. CRAIG GRAVEYARD
SMITH COUNTY

Located 2½ miles East of Carthage, Tenn., on North side of the
State Highway # 24, about 200 yards from Highway. Old Craig
farm now owned by Robert Arthur Waggoner.
Graveyard in good condition, has good fence.
Copied by Mrs. Cora W. Whitefield, Mrs. Bessie Gibbs, and Miss
Hattie Winfree, Carthage, Tennessee.
March 29, 1937.

L. B. Craig, Sr. (Mason)
Born Feb. 3, 1833.
Died June 7, 1900.
M. B. Craig,
Born May 10, 1887.
Died -----?
" An honest man the
noblest work of God."
M. M. Craig,
Born Nov. 18, 1845.
Died ----?
" Absent from the body,
Present with the Lord."
E. M. Craig,
Born Oct. 26, 1863.
Died Feb. 10, 1864.
S. S. Craig,
Born Jan. 13, 1864.
Died Nov. 5, 1866.
A.L. Craig,
Born June 16, 1867.
Died Jan. 18, 1886.
" Children though separated,
on earth, may we meet in
heaven."
B. M. Craig,
Born Feb. 18, 1882.
Died ----?
L. W. Craig,
Born May 8, 1884.
Died ----?
C. H. Craig,
Born Feb. 2, 1880.
Died Jan. 9, 1900.

E. L. Craig,
Born Jan. 8, 1876.
Died Apr. 17, 1907.
W. G. Craig,
Born Mar. 19, 1869.
Died Oct. 21, 1870.
L. B. Craig, Jr.
Born June 7, 1871.
Died ----?
C. S. Craig,
Born July 21, 1873.
Died ----?
B. B. Craig,
Born Nov. 11, 1888.
Died ----?

Lovingly Erected by Mrs.
L. B. Craig, 1901.

(Undertakers Marker)
B. B. Craig,
Died Mar. 21, 1933.
Age 54-4 mo. 11 days.

Infant son of Walter &
Mattie L. Ward,
Born Dec. 9, 1885.

Mattie Lee, Wife of
Walter W. Ward,
Born June 16, 1867.
Died Jan. 18, 1886.
"Since thou canst no
longer stay, To cheer me
with thy love; I hope
to meet with thee again,
In yon bright world above."

SMITH COUNTY

TOMBSTONE INSCRIPTIONS

DIXON SPRINGS   CEMETERY

Copied by Mrs. Bessie Gibbs, Dixon Springs, Tennessee, Apr. 19, 1937.

NEVILLE
Erline Wright wife of
Earl Neville
June 24, 1910 - Feb. 10, 1936

LANKFORD
Rheu Allen Lankford
Dec. 23, 1932 - Dec. 23, 1935

John P. Merryman
Died June 13, 1936
Age 82 yr. 6 mo. 27 days

Albert Clarence Gregory
May 26, 1909 - Dec. 21, 1935
"We shall meet again."

GREGORY
Joe G. Gregory
Oct. 25, 1903 - Aug. 21, 1934
"The sunshine of our home."
Joe Gregory Jr.
Mar. 2, 1934 - June 4, 1934
"Our Darling."

Jose B. Gann
Died Nov. 26, 1934
Age 71 yrs.   4 mos.

GREGORY
Earl A. Gregory
Mar. 4, 1914 - Apr. 7, 1935

COX
James Martin Cox
Feb. 4, 1868 - Apr. 2, 1936

Willie Brim
Feb. 6, 1919 - Feb. 5, 1934

Susan A. Brooks
Oct. 22, 1851
June 16, 1930
Mother

Charlie G. Brooks
Aug. 6, 1845
Nov. 13, 1918
Father

BROOKS

Delia T.   James H.
1872-1934   1869-1936

GARRISON
Thomas J. (his wife) Tennie Moss
1856-19___   1858-1929

Lula White More
June 12, 1883-Feb. 18, 1918
"Earth has no sorrow that heaven
cannot heal."

Esther Merryman
Born Sept. 4, 1825
Died Aug. 23, 1904
"Her happy soul has winged its
way to one pure, bright
eternal day."

J. P. Merryman
Born Mar. 7, 1823
Died _____
"His spirit smiles from that
bright shore and softly
whispers weep no more."

L. L. Johnson
Born Jan. 9, 1857
Age 55 yrs. 6 mo.

B. F. Crain
Died Feb. 4, 1925 Age 68 yrs.
"A tribute of love by
Pole Beasley and family."

Lucy wife of
Lieut. Jno. T. Montgomery

Lieut. Jno. T. Montgomery
A Confederate Soldier

A Board
Bearing Inscription
"Bob"

Mrs. Mary Tunstall
Born Aug. 22, 1833 Died Aug. 3, 1895
"She was a believer in and a
follower of the teachings of Christ."

"We shall meet again."
Charlie S. H. Tunstall
Born May 22, 1818-Died July 11, 1885
"Affliction sore long time I bore
Physicians' skill in vain,
Till Christ was pleased to give
me ease and rid me of my pain.
(Brown, Albany Ind.)"

Bud Gregory
Born Jan. 1863, Died Apr. 4, 1914
"Meet me in heaven."

COX
William Henry Cox
May 29, 1853-Jan. 6, 1919
Elizabeth D. Cox
Mar. 3, 1854-May 18, 1920
Edgar Cox
Sept. 1883 -Aug. 6, 1884
"God gave, He took, he will restore,
He doeth all things well."

Henry H. Cox
Born May 11, 1822-Died Mar. 14, 1905
"An honest man the noblest work of God."

In Memory of Aunt Jemima
Faithful servant of Henry H. Cox & Family
1820 - June 8, 1883

Sacred in the memory of
Sallie daut. of H. H. & F. M.
Cox Born May 11, 1865
Died June 15, 1873

Nancy French wife of
Henry H. Cox
Febry. 5, 1826- Oct. 12, 1862

Mattie Duke
Nov. 20, 1858 - Apr. 18, 1933

Gladys Organ
wife of H. H. White
Sept. 4, 1894 - Jan. 11, 1916
"Just when we learned to love her
most, God called her back to
heaven."

WHITE
George W. White   Sarah E. White
1858-19____   1859-1931

Wade Gregory
Mar. 5, 1881 - May 4, 1925

Theda Belle Gregory dau. of
Wade & Bertha Gregory
Feb. 10, 1918 - Mar. 3, 1918

Beatrice Estell Buchanon
Mar. 15, 1935 Age 74 yr. 5 mo.
10 days

Sarah F. Merryman
July 15, 1860
July 23, 1920
Mother
David J. Merryman
Apr. 8, 1858
Apr. 13, 1926
Father
"Be ye ready for in such an hour
as ye think not the son of man
cometh."

William Stalcup
Feb. 28, 1844 - Mar. 21, 1910

William A. Stalcup
Nov. 25, 1885 - Jan. 7, 1909

Jennie Jones wife of R. A. Norris
1880   -   1925

JONES
James Banks Jones
Jan. 7, 1833 - Feb. 13, 1917)
)
    Susan Hughes Jones   )
May 6, 1845 - Nov. 14, 1915)

Cornelia A. Jones
wife of Neil A.   Beck
Aug. 29, 1875 - Jan. 9, 1909

Nevada L. Jones
Born Mar. 26, 1873-Died Feb. 1, 1892
"He giveth his beloved sleep."

Sula Jones wife of A. W. Gann
1887   -   1925

Lizzie K. Stevens wife of
J. E. Stevens
Born Sept. 30, 1840, Died June 23, 1870

Jones E. Stevens
Aug. 31, 1841 - Mar. 11, 1882

Emily Stevens
1868   -   1902

Lucy V. Jolley
Born Mar. 25, 1854, Died Oct. 25, 1890
"In God's own world her orb will rise
once more a star of Paradise."

"Blessed are the dead,which live in
the Lord."
Holy Bible
Mary A. wife of J. E. Haynie
Born Aug. 1, 1838, Died Jan. 25, 1874
"A loving wife and mother dear
in sweet repose is sleeping here
Her painful loss we deeply feel
But God can all our sorrows heal."

(Note: Mrs. Oakley Knight buried here
        July 1934. Information by:
        Mr. Bill Corum, Riddleton, Tenn.)

KENNEDY
(Marker with no inscriptions)

(Note: Mrs. Wade Anderson
            buried here-no marker-
Died Apr. 19, 1937 Age 56 yrs.
Information by Mr. Bill Corum,
Riddleton, Tenn.) (Error. Mrs. Wade Anderson is still
living in Gallatin, Tenn. aged 90
this day 1960 L.S.S.

(Note: Benton Jolly a soldier
            of World War
Buried here - no marker -
Information by Mrs. Agnes
Garrett Young, Dixon Springs,
Tenn.)

Bryan Gregory
Jan. 15, 1902 - Jan. 8, 1934
"Just in the morning of his day
in youth & Love he died."

Odell   Jewell   M.W.A.
June 9, 1906 Jan. 1,1909
Nov. 7, 1918 Mar.25,1932
"In heaven   "His memory
 there is one   is Blessed."
 angel more."
        JONES

Lucy P. Clariday
July 17, 1904-Mar. 11, 1924
"Earth contains a mortal loss,
Heaven an angel more."

W. D. Porter his wife Lizzie Porter
Feb. 16, 1868   July 28, 1871
                     Aug. 5, 1930
_____

Jessie L.   Mary T.
Mar. 14, 1871   Oct. 30, 1872
July 6, 1931
"Gone but not
 forgotten."   "We will meet again."
        GREGORY
William Edward Eliza Adline
Feb. 10, 1866   July 12, 1867
         19___   Aug. 7, 1936

David B. Wright
Nov. 30, 1904 - Apr. 3, 1935

Jno. M. Harrison
A Confederate Soldier

Thomas Petty
A Confederate Soldier

Thomas Dias
Soldier of War 1812

Thomas Williams
1861 - 1927

Elizabeth Williams
1866 - _____
(Note: Dead but date of
death unknown.)

Elizabeth Gregoty wife of
Z. T. Gregory
Born Nov. 11, 1849-Died Jan. 10, 1901
GREGORY

"Father at rest"
D. Briggs Mintz
Born Nov. 21, 1875-Died Sept. 10, 1910

Lydia Jane Mintz
Born Feb. 24, 1878-Died Nov. 3, 1898
"Our darling one hath gone before to
greet us on the blissful shore."

Mary M. Mintz	W. M. Mintz
July 21, 1841	Born Oct. 30, 1822
Sep. 11, 1917	Died Sep. 26, 1902
"A loving wife	"An honest man,
a mother dear	the noblest work
lies buried here."	of God."

A tribute to Smith County's pioneers
Salvation Army   Y.M.C.A.   Preachers,
Boy Scouts,   Red Cross   War Boards
Loyal Men   Patriotic Women
Gov. Tom C. Rye
Woodrow Wilson

Soldiers who sleep here   Confederate Soldiers
Soldiers of all wars.
Gen. N. B. Forrest
Gen. Robt. E. Lee

WORLD WAR
Smith Ctys. world war Gold stars-

Chas. R. Baird	Frank Davis
Jno. C. Hazzard	Sidney Flatt
Ben S. High	Will D. Hunt
Robt. Jennings	Jas. E.Ledford
Frank Manning	Wm. C. Marks
Andrew Nunely	Jas. Odum
Lem B. Nabors	Chas. E. Price
Elbert Richardson	Thos.K.Stallings
Horace Webb	Benton Winkler
G. S. McGuffee	Y.M.C.A. Socty.

Brownlow Cowan Col.
Jas. Vaughn Col.

A. W. Williams (Mason)
Born Nov. 28, 1817, Died July 22, 1874
"A faithful husband and father dear,
In sweet repose is sleeping here,
His painful loss we deeply feel,
But God can all our sorrows heal."

Nancy wife of Edward
Stovall
Died Jan. 2, 1861 Aged about 65
years

John A. son of A. W. & J. F.
Williams
Born May 26, 1856, Died Oct. 6,1857

John S. son of A. W. & J. F.
Williams
Born July 9, 1853, Died Dec. 27,1853

L. A. son of L. A. &
Cordie Culley
Nov. 28, 1922 - May 2, 1924
"Budded on earth to bloom in
heaven."

Thos. T. Stovall
Born Mar. 5, 1819 Died Jan. 26,
1894
"Asleep in Jesus."
God gave, he took, he will
restore
He doeth all things well."

Mary Katherine Ferguson
wife of Thos. K. Stovall
1839   -   1915

Leonard Ballow
Born May 5, 1800 Died Jan. 17, 1869
(J. S. Clark Co. Lou. Ky.)

Jane N. Ballow
Born Nov. 11, 1812 Died Dec. 23, 1887

Minerva J. Ballow
Born June 13, 1858 Died Dec. 3, 1898

Mary L. Ballow
Born Mar. 6, 1835 Died Sept. 30, 1917

Edward T. Denny
Feb. 5, 1891
"God's finger touched him and he slept."

James L. Alexander
Son of Richard & Nancy Alexander
Born Oct. 24, 1817 Died Aug. 5, 1895
"I am the resurrection and the life."
John XL   25-5

Sarah Donoho wife of
James L. Alexander
Born Apr. 17, 1826 Died Feb. 1, 1904
"For thou art my hope O! Lord, God!
Thou art my trust from my youth."
ALEXANDER

Goldman Donoho Alexander
Born June 24, 1849 Died Jan. 3, 1909
"Blessed are they that take refuge
in him."

ALEXANDER
Walter Clinton   1846 - 1927

ALEXANDER
Nannie Ellis
1869 - 1928

Our Baby
Annalee Robertson
Mar. 8, 1900   -   July 15, 1903

Cinda Gregory   William Gregory
Dec. 31, 1865   Jan. 23, 1865.
                        May 16, 1930
                "Gone but not forgotten."

Mother   Father

Luther Gregory
Nov. 4, 1867   -   Oct. 9, 1935
"Blessed"

Ella Lee Dau. of Bill &
Cinda Gregory
wife of Carsey Porter
Jan. 27, 1903 - June 19, 1919
"Beneath this stone lies the
body of a noble daughter,
a true Christian, a precious
wife and a loving mother she
sweetly sleeps in Jesus."

WILLIAMS
Anne L. Williams   W. T. Williams
Jan. 7, 1872   Dec. 5, 1847
July 17,1916   Mar.12, 1924

Margiania E. Lipscomb
wife of W. T. Williams
Mar. 7, 1848 - Aug. 31, 1908

John Howard Allen Jr.
Infant 1918.

A
In loving memory

Clara V. Allen John D. Allen
Sept. 3, 1846   Mar. 29, 1835
July 22, 1914   Nov. 24, 1919
ALLEN

"Unforgotten"
George A. Howard son of Jacob &
Sarah Howard
1840-1900
"Endowed with a fine Intellect and
a pure heart, a stainless honor
crowned his life."

"Farewell till we meet again."
James T. Cox
Born Dec. 1, 1855 Died Dec.18,
1882
"He passed from our sight
like a dream or a story
from a bosom of love to a
mansion of glory.
(Brown N. Albany Ind.)"

Jane Lynch Cox
1831 - 1893
"Known unto God are all his works."

John C. Cox
Feb. 18, 1827 - Apr. 4, 1905

Vally Victoria daughter of
Cal & Molly Cox
Born Aug. 29, 1888-Died Oct. 16, 1888

Lucy Cox McPherson
1865 - May 7
1918 - Aug. 23
Wife of Campbell McPherson

Mattie Winkler   W. A. Winkler
Sept. 27, 1856   Feb. 11, 1861
                      Jan. 18, 1919
——————————— WINKLER

DILLAHA
C. V. D. Dillaha
May 1, 1868 - Nov. 12, 1934

One Stone
Virginia Wilson Martin
1905 - 1934
Anna Elizabeth
1877 - 1930
Thos. Wilson
1877 - 19____

Anna Mai Hackett
May 7, 1899 - Apr. 9, 1930
"Our loved one."

John Morris
Mar. 15, 1851
Feb. 20, 1929
"Freed"

Callie Hanye
Born Sept. 5, 1879 Died Feb. 2, 1902
"We loved her, yes we loved her,
but Angels loved her more."

Hanye
Marshall B.   His wife   Susie Bradley
1853-1924   1876-1935

Sarah A.
"She is freed from her labors,
and her works do follow her."
Holy Bible
Wife of H. B. Hanye
Born Feb. 11, 1821
Died June 4, 1891

"Blessed are the dead who
die in the Lord."
Holy Bible
Henry B. Hanye
Born Mar. 16, 1816
Died Dec. 7, 1881
Borwn N.   Albany Ind.

BOWMAN
Mai High wife of W. S. Bowman
Sept. 26, 1886-Feb. 11, 1924

Elizabeth Tennessee Maxey
Sept. 28, 1852
Oct. 10, 1932

William Beasley
Apr. 8, 1937
Age 76 yrs. 6 mo. 9 da.

James D. Turner   Mollie M. Turner
Jan. 27, 1860   Apr. 6, 1867
                    July 31,1930
Father   and   Mother

Alice Kindred Jones
Feb. 6, 1864-Nov. 30, 1928
"Asleep in Jesus."

Eugene Kindred
July 26, 1857-June 7, 1920
"Jesus loves the pure and holy."

Betty Burford Wright
wife of Romulus C. Wright
Born Sept. 21, 1832 Died Apr. 4,
1898
"A heart and mind of rarest mold,
An instinct true
Her soul found nature's streams of
gold and richly drew."

Romulus C. Wright
Born in Amelia Co. Va. 1818
Died at his home near Dixon's
Spring July 15, 1882
        Aged 74 yrs. & 5 mos.
"His life was gentle and the elements
  so mixed, stand up and say to all
  the world "This was a man."

YOUNG

William Martin Young Jr.
        1892 - 1924
        Served in France
        1918 - 1919
        605th Engineers

        his wife
Agnes Garret 1890-
          etc. ?

Sam Martin Young Senr.
May 29, 1861 - Mar. 19, 1935
"He loved his fellow man."
        His wife
        Elizabeth A. Wright
        Jan. 1, 1865

YOUNG

Addison H. Young
Born June 4, 1846 Died May 9, 1919
"Blessed is he that maketh the Lord
  his trust."

Sallie Wright Young
Born Apr. 18, 1858 Died July 10, 1913
"Behold we count them happy what
  endure."

In memory of
Harriet Wright Lowe
Born June 10, 1829 Died Nov. 2, 1898
"Truth fidelity and usefulness
  Weave a crown of honor about her
  memory."

Nova Brimm Kennedy
May 17, 1936 Aged 50 yrs. 3 months.

Richard Edward C. Kennedy
Apr. 24, 1909   -   Aug. 15, 1925

Elijah Rollins
Dec. 20, 1892 -   Nov. 10, 1918
"Since thou can no longer stay
  To cheer me with thy love
I hope to meet with thee again,
  In yon bright world above."

Sadie Agnes Rollins
Born Aug. 3, 1894 Died May 17,1904
"Her spirit smiles from that
  bright shore,
And softly whispers weep no more."

Monroe T. son of
J. D. & Josie Rollins
Born Dec. 13, 1886 Died June 4,
        1888
"Goodby my darling child Till we
  meet again."

Josie Dau. of Julia Mai
        Rollins
Sept. 1, 1916 - Jan. 10, 1919
"Sleep on sweet babe and take thy
  rest
God called thee home, he thought
  it best."

Brice Shoulders, Jr.
Jan. 30, 1929 - June 27, 1932
"Gone but not forgotten."

DYCUS
William A. Dycus Nov.18,1844
July 22, 1925. A Confederate
        Soldier.

HIX
Hester Coe
March 19, 1901 - Jan. 23, 1919

Ellen Katherine Dycus
Feb. 23, 1857 - July 7, 1925

BALLOU
Tennessee Bowman
Wife of Ward Ballou
1851 - 1925

R. C. (Ward) Ballou
A Confederate Soldier
1847 - 1907

Mary Frances Jordan
June 13, 1901 - Apr. 5, 1908
"God keeps, her safe through his eternal
  years."

T. Ethel Carter
Born May 13, 1908 Died May 13, 1909

BROWN
Joseph H. His wife Nancy J. Nelson
1858-1927   1862-1911
"Beloved ones farewell."

Mrs. Maggie Brown Carter
Died May 20, 1935
Aged 46 yrs. 4 mos. 25 days.

Albert Bowman   (Mason)
Born May 9, 1872- Died Dec. 5, 1909
"Beneath this stone in soft repose
Is laid a Mother's dearest child
BOWMAN

BOWMAN

Father   Mother
James Pope   Martha Brim
1838-1917   1849-____
A Confederate Soldier

Bowman

William Bullard
Nov. 1, 1844 - Jan. 22, 1914
"His toils are past, His work is done,
He fought the fight, the victory won."

Cora Susan Ballou
Born Mar. 7, 1877-Died Aug. 28, 1930
"Her happy soul has winged its way to
one bright eternal day."
BALLOU

Father
T. B. Allen
Dec. 4, 1868   -   June 25, 1920
"He is not dead but sleepeth."

Mother
Sidney Allen
Feb. 15, 1871 - Feb. 14, 1920
"Her end was peace."

HANYE
Josephene Graves   N. B. Hanye
wife of N. B. Hanye Born Jan. 25, 1836
1845-1888   Died Apr. 10, 1912

Anis L. Johnson 1865-1934

H. L. Johnson   1864-1927

One Stone
Charles Swope   Mary Swope
Feb. 25, 1848   Feb. 8, 1860
Aug. 17, 1923   _____

Hugh Bradley Wright)
1866 - 1929   )
Elizabeth Black Wright)
1866 - 19____   )

Charles E. Black
Apr. 13, 1874 - Sept. 18, 1917

Sarah E. Thompson wife
of David C. Black
Born Feb. 23, 1835
Died Dec. 27, 1923

David C. Black
Born Nov. 12, 1839
Died June 17, 1905
"Sheltered and safe from sorrow."

Mollie Brazier
Mar. 26, 1865
Sept. 25, 1928

John Elvir Debow son
of John L. & Elvir Debow
Born Aug. 16, 1887
Died June 2, 1905
"His mercy endureth forever."

John L. Debow Son of
Archibald and Sallie Debow
1853 - 1900
"When I awake in His likeness
I shall be Satisfied."
Foot Rock:
"He wore the white flower of a
pure kind life."

Tabitha Law
wife of N. B. Hanye
1844-1909

* * *

TOMBSTONE - INSCRIPTIONS

DYER GRAVEYARD
SMITH COUNTY

Located about one-fourth mile from the Court House, West of
Carthage, Tennessee. They are badly in need of repair.
Soldiers were buried here, but were moved to Nashville, Tenn.
Copied by Mrs. Bessie Gibbs and Miss Hattie Ferrell Winfree,
Carthage, Tennessee.
March 5, 1937.

Joel Dyer,
Born in N.C.
Died in Carthage,
Nov. 14, 1836. Served
in Legislature in 1809.
Senate in 1815-1821.
Erected by Matilda V. James,
1856.

Mrs. Mary H. Dyer, Wife of
Joel Dyer, Daughter of
Daniel Burford & Elizabeth Hawkins,
Born Oct. 14, 1779.(?)
Died Dec. 11, 1806.
Erected by Matilda James, 1856.

TOMBSTONE - INSCRIPTIONS

POLLY GIBBS GRAVEYARD
SMITH COUNTY

Located near Gordonsville, Tennessee. Take road that leaves
Carthage, Tenn,to Gordonsville 2½ miles, turn left ½ mile,on
farm now owned by Mrs. Mary Winfree.
The graveyard is in poor condition and has no fence.
There are about 100 unmarked graves.
Copied by Miss Hattie Winfree and Mrs. Bessie Gibbs.
March 29, 1937.

Hezzie Kay Meadows,
Sept. 15, 1884.
May 1, 1910.
" Though thou art gone,
Fond memory clings in thee"

France Thaxton,
Apr. 3, 1832.
Mar. 13, 1920.

(Undertakers Marker)
Arah Boulton,
Died Feb. 9, 1927.
1-11 mo. 9 da.

Azzie Lee, Wife of
H. B. Lynch,
Sept. 6, 1888.
Feb. 15, 1917.
" Asleep in Jesus"

Frances Lynch,
Born Apr. 29, 1853.
Died Dec. 14, 1912.
"At Rest"

(Undertakers Marker)
Clarence Gibbs,
Apr. 30, 1930.
47 yrs.3 mo.19 da.

(Undertakers Marker)
Evaline Smith Gibbs,
Aug. 19, 1922.
Age. 62 yrs.5 mo.19 da.

Bennet Gibbs,
Jan. 17, 1925.
Age 72 yrs. 22 da.

G. W. Lynch,
Born June 12, 1824.
Died Sept. 16, 1907.
"Earth has no sorrow,
Heaven cannot heal"

Mary,Wife of
Geo. W. Lynch,
Feb. 27, 1836.
Dec. 5, 1918.
Age 82 yrs.9 mo.8 da.
"She was a kind and affectionate
wife & mother,and a friend
to all."

Maggie, Wife of
J. H. Boulton,
Born Sept. 22, 1886.
Died Sept. 11, 1908.

(Polly Gibbs Graveyard p.2.)

Henry D. Gass,
Born Dec. 4, 1816.
Died Dec. 19, 1894.
"Since thou cans't no longer
stay to cheer me with thy
love, I hope to meet with
thee again in yon bright
world above."

Infant daughter of
J. C. & M. E. Gibbs.

Susie, Wife of
J. R. Jarrard,
Born Oct. 9, 1854.
Died Apr. 16, 1886.
"Sleep Susie sleep,
Thy toils are o'er;
Sweet be thy rest,
So oft needed before,
Well have I loved you,
But God loved you more,
Has called you now to
that bright happy shore."

James W.,Son of
J. R. & Susie Jarrard,
Born Oct. 22, 1883.
Died Feb. 8, 1885.

MOTHER:
Martha E. Gibbs,
Born June 22, 1850.
Died Aug. 26, 1924.
FATHER:
James C. Gibbs,
-Born Jan. 7, 1844.
Died Dec. 28, 1926.
"Since thou can no longer
stay to cheer me with
thy love;I hope to meet with
thee again,In yon bright
world above."

John Gibbs,
Born Sept. 19, 1816.
Died Jan. 25, 1879/
"A loving husband, a
father dear;
A faithful friend
lies buried here."

Mary Gibbs, Wife of
John Gibbs,
Born Mar. 20, 1814.
Died Nov. 30, 1906.
"Gone but not forgotten".

TOMBSTONE - INSCRIPTIONS

GLOVER GRAVEYARD
SMITH COUNTY

Located about 5 miles from Carthage, Tenn.,leaving Carthage,
cross the Cordell Hull Bridge, turn left on Highway No. 70,
keep straight road, cross Caney Fork Bridge,and turn to left,
first side road, 1 mile on right side of road.
Graveyard in fair condition, no fence.
There are 5 un marked graves.
Copied by Miss Hattie Winfree and Mrs. Bessie Gibbs.
March 29, 1937.

Margaret R. Dau. of
J. & S. Beasley,
Born Aug. 28, 1857.
Died Sept. 22, 1858.

Martha J.,Dau. of
J. & S. Beasley,
Born Mar. 2, 1839.
Died Aug. 16, 1840.

Jesse Beasley,
Born Oct. 8, 1812.
Died Feb. 3, 1884.
" Not lost,but gone Home."

John W. Glover,
Nov. 14, 1842.
Jan. 27, 1920.
" I have fought a good fight,
I have finished my course,
I have kept the faith."

Martha F. Glover,
Aug. 28, 1877.
Feb. 19, 1899.
"We will meet again."

William E. Glover,
Aug. 30, 1880.
Oct. 20, 1902.
"Our Loved One."

SMITH COUNTY

TOMBSTONE - INSCRIPTIONS
HAILEY GRAVEYARD

The Hailey Graveyard is located beside the Williams & Wilson Grave-
yard, about 7 miles from Carthage, Tennessee. Leaving Carthage cross the
Cordull Hull bridge, turn to the right and travel about 7 miles. This
graveyard is on a hill between the little towns of Rome and Rock City.
It is about one hundred yards from the highway and can easily be seen from
the highway. There are 3 unmarked graves on the outside of the fence.
Copied by Miss Mattie M. Jones, Carthage, Tennessee - Route # 2.
October 1937.

Mrs. Betty Marks
Died March 9, 1937
Age 68 years - 4 mo. & 13 days
(Marker)

TOMBSTONE - INSCRIPTIONS

HART GRAVEYARD
SMITH COUNTY

This grave is located in Carthage, Tenn.,about one block
from the Court house, on the left side of Main Street.
There is one grave with no tombstone,beside this grave;
(Wm. Hart is buried here. This information was given by Mrs.
Allie Swope, Carthage, Tennessee.)
Copied by Miss Hattie Winfree, Carthage, Tennessee.
March 5, 1937.

In Memoriam,
Catharine E. Hart,Daughter of
Peter & Catharine Jones,
Born in Amelia County, Vt., Vn
23rd July, 1799.
Married to Wm. Hart,
29th August, 1816.
Died in Carthage, Tenn.,
2nd November, 1854.

"Reqiescat in Pace."

SMITH COUNTY

TOMBSTONE INSCRIPTIONS

HICKMAN GRAVEYARD

Located in town of Hickman, Tennessee.
One old tomb not marked, built of large stones.
Copied 1935.

Chesley Ray
Born June 3, 1839 Died
June 27,1897

S. A. Pittross wife of
Chesley Ray Born Aug. 16, 1838
Died Sept. 15, 1888

Narcissa K.,
Wife of Andrew J. Garrison
Born June 19, 1832
Died ____ 29, 1888

Wm.(?) K. Williams
Born Jan. 23, 1839 Died 1897 (?)

Martha S. wife of
J. B. Mason
Born Jan. 10, 1854, Died Oct. 7, 1889

Martha Denney Aged 86 years
(No Dates)

Mollie M. Newbill
Born 1828 - Died 1889

Lueller, Dau.(?) of C. W. & M. A.(?)
Newbill
Born Jan. 10, 1830, Died Oct. 26, 1892

Frances E. dau. of T. M. &
Mary Jane Ward, Born 1855
Died Feb. 14, 1873

Evaline Thomas
Born Oct. 8, 1821, Died Aug. 11, 1884

James Thomas, Born Dec. 2, 1811;
Died July 16, 1875

James B. Son of
J. & E. Thomas
Born Sept. 3, 1852
Died Feb. 14, 1874

Wm. Son of
J. & M. Prescott
Born Jan. 11, 1846;
Died July 1, 1867

G. G. Thomas
Born Sept. 28, 1846
Died June 10, 1906

Lucy Jane Hughes
Born Apr. 26, 1841
Died July 28, 1921

C. P. Hughes
Born Oct. 11, 1832
Died Mar. 4, 1893

Sarah E. wife of
F. F. Gwaltney
Born July 13, 1846
Died Oct. 5, 1886

A. H. Hughes
Sept. 30, 1858
Aug. 17, 1925.
His Wife
P. F. Agee Hughes
Feb. 26, 1859, Nov. 28, 1933

Barthany Russell
Mar. 23, 1845, Mar. 29, 1918

Elder M. W. Russell
Feb. 6, 1845 - Feb. 22, 1914.

* * *

TOMBSTONE - INSCRIPTIONS

HODGES GRAVEYARD
SMITH COUNTY

Located about ¼ mile from Highway No. 70, on left, about one
mile from Carthage, Tennessee.
The graveyard is in fair condition.
There are 20 graves with rocks, but no inscriptions.
Copied by Mrs. Bessie Gibbs and Miss Hattie Winfree, Carthage,
Tennessee.
March 31, 1937.

Jordan N. Williams,
Born Nov. 3, 1835.
Died Aug. 6, 1874.
"A loving husband,
A father dear; A
faithful friend,
lies buried here."

Mary B., Dau. of,
J. N. & L. V. Williams,
Born Nov. 7, 1873.
Died Dec. 21, 1886.
"Beneath this stone,
In soft repose, Is
laid a mother's
dearest pride; A
flower that scarce
had wait to life and
light and beauty,
Ere it died."

Richard Hodges,
Born July 17, 1862.
Died Aug. 7, 1906.
"Asleep in Jesus,
Blessed Sleep; From
which none ever wake,
To weep."

POPE:
Lily Hodges Pope,
Born Mar. 31, 1873.
Died Feb. 2, 1916.
"A loving wife, a mother dear,
Lies buried here."

LOVE:
Amy B. Hodges,
Born May 15, 1837.
Died Nov. 25, 1911.
"Thy trials ended,
Thy rest is won."

David P. Hodges,
Born Aug. 12, 1810.
Died Nov. 1, 1900.

Martha, Wife of,
C. S. Robinson,
Nov. 22, 1887.
Jan. 6, 1910.
ROBINSON:

Horace P. Lawhorn,
Mar. 11, 1913.
Aug. 7, 1913.
"Budded on earth,
To bloom in heaven."

"At Rest"
Ferd A. Lawhorn,
- June 2, 1902.
Nov. 3, 1918.
"A precious one from
us has gone, A voice
we loved is stilled;
A place is vacant in
our home, That never
can be filled."

TOMBSTONE - INSCRIPTIONS

WEST HUGHES GRAVEYARD
SMITH COUNTY

Located ¼ mile on left of Highway No. 70, two miles from
Carthage, Tenn.,and about 300 yards from point where Caney
Fork River runs into Cumberland River. Farm is now owned by
daughter of West Hughes; Mrs. Lyda Green, Old Hickory, Tennessee.
Graveyard is in bad condition and has no fence.
There are 15 unmarked graves.
Copied by Mrs. Bessie Gibbs, Carthage, Tennessee.
March 29, 1937.

Pachal Elworth Lawhorn,
Born Aug. 29, 1906.
Died Feb. 29, 1909.
" Budded on earth,
To bloom in heaven."

Jas. T. Duncan,
Born Aug. 14, 1867.
June 9, 1927.
" Asleep in Jesus."

TOMBSTONE - INSCRIPTIONS

KNIGHT GRAVEYARD
SMITH COUNTY

Located in Chestnut Mound, Tennessee, about 10 miles from
Carthage, Tenn., on Highway # 70. Poorly fenced.
Joins farm now owned by Howard McDonald.
One unmarked grave.
Copied by Mrs. Cora Whitefield, Carthage, Tennessee.
March 29, 1937.

Walton Fain Cooper,
Born Nov. 12, 1912.
Died Nov. 13, 1912.

Samuel F.,Son of
E. H. & Eliza Knight,
Born Dec. 26, 1878.
Died July 21, 1891.

"At Rest"
Robert H. Knight,
Born Nov. 22, 1875.
Died Apr. 8, 1904.
"An honest man, the
noblest work of God."

Dr. Elijah Haynie Knight,
Aug. 20, 1841.
May 26, 1923.
"None knew but to love thee,
None named thee,but to praise."
His Wife,
Eliza Fain Knight,
Sept. 17, 1852.

Robert W. Knight,
Born Oct. 24, 1811.
Died Dec. 14, 1896.
"Erected to the memory
of father and mother,
By their children."

Susan Haynie, Wife of
R. W. Knight,
Born Aug. 20, 1818.
Died Jan. 13, 1903.

Fannie Mahaney Knight,
July 20, 1862.
Sept. 25, 1927.
"A loving wife, a mother
dear, Lies buried here."

H. L. Knight,
Oct. 22, 1852.
"An honest man, the noblest
work of God."

TOMBSTONE - INSCRIPTIONS

MAFIELD GRAVEYARD
SMITH COUNTY

Located in a lot on the left side of the Alvin C. York High-
way # 24, about three miles from Carthage, Tennessee, on the
Lebanon Road. It is about 200 yards from the Highway.
There are about 15 graves with rocks, but no inscriptions.
Graveyard is in poor condition.
Copied by Mrs. Bessie Gibbs and Miss Hattie Winfree.
March 31, 1937.

Jessie May Harris,
Born May 2, 1923.
Died Jan. 18, 1926.
" Gone but not forgotten."

Mary Lou, Dau.of
R. A. & J. E. Ward,
Born Jan. 27, 1890.
Died May 15, 1890.
" Budded on earth,
To bloom in heaven."

W. A. Poindexter,
Died Feb. 21, 1918.
Age 38 yrs.
" Gone but not forgotten."

SMITH COUNTY

TOMBSTONE RECORDS

McCLURES BEND CEMETERY

This cemetery is located about 3½ miles East from Defeated on John M. Robinson Farm. This land was given for this purpose by Landy Robinson. Copied by Rebecca Ballenger September 2, 1936.

Mrs. Barbara Allison May 31, 1842 May 28, 1928

Landy Robinson Feb. 13, 1849 Mar. 16, 1917

James J. Robinson Sept. 14, 1850 July 5, 1926

John M. Robinson Jan. 18, 1818 May 19, 1874

Sarah B. Robinson June 15, 1819 May 3, 1898

Aletha F. Shoemake Sept. 3, 1835 Apr. 2, 1909

Miles Shoemake Mar. 15, 1823 Mar. 13, 1895

Sallie A. Williamson Jan. 18, 1856 Mar. 23, 1915

TOMBSTONE - INSCRIPTIONS

OLD McDONALD GRAVEYARD
SMITH COUNTY

Located 2 miles from Gordonsville, Tennessee, ¼ mile on left
of Highway or road leading to New Middleton, Tennessee.
From Carthage, Tennessee, cross Cordell Hull Bridge, across
Cumberland River, turn to left ¾ mile, turn right on Gordons-
ville Road 5 miles, turn to right on New Middleton Road 2 miles,
graveyard is ¼ mile from road at the foot of what is known as
Whitley Hill.
First owner: Henry McDonald, 2nd owner: E. M. McDonald.
Present owner: Henry C. Orange.
There are 5 unmarked graves.
Note:(Henry McDonald & wife, Lucinda Watkins McDonald, and
Martha Prentice are buried here, no marker. Information given
by grand-daughter of Henry McDonald, Mrs.Sophia McDonald Agee,
Gordonsville, Tennessee. Star #)
Copied by Mrs. Bessie Gibbs, Carthage, Tennessee.
May 31, 1937.

Lela Eastes, Wife of
J. M. McDonald,
July 15, 1878.
Jan. 16, 1907.

John Eastes McDonald,
Born Aug. 28, 1899.
Died Apr. 25, 1913.
" Beneath this stone in
soft repose, Is hid a
mother's dearest pride."

Anna Lee McDonald,
Born Dec. 24, 1912.
Died Oct. 12, 1913.
" Budded on earth,to
bloom in heaven."

LOVE:
Julia A.,Wife of
S. B. Thomas,
Jan. 3, 1864.
Oct. 29, 1880.
" A tender mother,
A faithful friend."
THOMAS:

E. M. McDonald,

(E.M.McDonald cont.)
E. M. McDonald,
Aug. 13, 1840.
May 24, 1915.
"Weep not,he is at Rest."
MCDONALD:

Elizabeth, Wife of
E. M. McDonald,
Aug. 16, 1844.
Aug. 7, 1919.
"Farewell sweet mother,
Thou shall ever be,
A star to guide us up
to heaven, and to thee."
MCDONALD.

W. L. McDonald,
Nov. 18, 1861.
Feb. 14, 1927.
Age 65 years,2 mo. 26 days.
" Dearest brother,thou hast
left us here; Thy loss we
deeply feel;But 'tis God that
hath bereft us, He can all
our sorrows heal."
MCDONALD.

SMITH COUNTY

TOMBSTONE INSCRIPTIONS

POINDEXTER GRAVEYARD

Located 200 yards from the main highway, 3 miles from Carthage, Tennessee.
15 Graves are unmarked.

Jessie May Harris
Born May 2, 1923
Died Jan. 18, 1926
"Gone but not forgotten."

Mary Lou Dau. of
R. H. & J. E. Ward
Born Jan. 27, 1890
Died May 15, 1890
"Budded on earth to bloom
in heaven."

W. A. Poindexter
Died Feb. 21, 1918
Age 38 yrs.
"Gone but not forgotten."

*   *   *

TOMBSTONE - INSCRIPTIONS

RIDGEWOOD CEMETERY
SMITH COUNTY

Located about one-half mile due East of Carthage,Tennessee.
The road that leads to the Cemetery is known as the "Old
Walton Trail".
There are about 65 unmarked graves in this Cemetery.
Copied by Mrs. Cora Whitefield,Mrs.Bessie Gibbs,and Miss
Hattie Winfree, Carthage, Tennessee.
March 5, 1937.

James C. Sanders,
Born Nov. 17, 1812.
Died Jan. 20, 1903.
Age 90 yrs.2 mo.3 days.

Malvina Titald Sanders,
Born April 18, 1832.
Married July 4, 1850.
Died April 17, 1883.
Age 50 years,11 mos.29 days.

(Undertakers Marker.)
Charlie W. Chilcutt,
Died Feb. 27, 1937.
Age 60 yrs.4 mo.27 days.

William B. Bryant,
Aug. 1861-Sept. 26,1929.
"Asleep in Jesus,Blessed
thought."

Bessie Scudders Savage,
June 6, 1889-Apr.26, 1921.
"Gods voice across the storm
called her home,in him
she lives."

F. P. McGinness,
July 5, 1849,
Feb. 28,   ,

William Housten McGinness,
Oct. 9, 1925,
Nov. 6, 1929/

Virgil Lee McGinness,
Mar. 18, 1836,
Sept. 11, 1907.

MATHEWS:
John W. & Carsie L.
Sept.2,1920,-June 18, 1922,
Oct. 20,1935.Oct. 20, 1935.
Newsboys-Brothers,Killed on
their way to deliver papers.

WEBB:
Horace Hale,
1898-1918.
Died in France,A.E.F.
Wilhelm Kerr,
June 13, 1868,
Feb. 7, 1936.

Volina M. Manning,
1916-1936.

Louis Winston Stone,
Aug. 25, 1927.
Nov. 11, 1933.
"Sleep on, sweet babe,and
take thy rest, God called
thee home, He thought it
best."

Annie Francis Jordan,
Born Jan. 25, 1936.
Died Feb. 2, 1936.
"Gone,but not forgotten."

Grace L. Ragland,
March 24, 1896.
Jan. 23, 1920.
" And with farewell
unspoken, she calmly
entered Home."

(Undertakers Marker.)
Nellie Elizabeth
(Timberlake) Winfree,
Died Feb. 1, 1937.
Age 52 yrs.4 mo.28 days.
Born Oct.3, 1884.
Married A.C. Winfree,
Sept. 27, 1907.

J. M. Williford,
Jan. 18, 1924.
Age about 92 yrs.
" God gave,He took,
He will restore,
He doeth all things well."

Jennie Pettie,
Oct. 12, 1889.
Apr.12, 1930.
" Our Loved One."

FORD-
Father:
Rev. M. N. Ford,
Mar. 15, 1844.
Jan. 23, 1898. 1928
MOTHER:
Frances F. Ford,
Aug. 24, 1845.
Apr. 2, 1925.
" Our Fondest hopes
Lie buried here."

FORD:
W. B. Ford,
Aug. 13, 1866.
Dec. 10, 1932.

McKinney Swope,
Apr. 15, 1859.
Jan. 2, 1936.

Roy Thomas Arnold,
Dec. 21, 1931.
Mar. 12, 1933.
" Asleep in Jesus."

J. T. Gann,
Jan. 29, 1905.
Aug. 5, 1931.
"His Memory is Blessed."

Ollie Gibbs,Wife of
J. N. Gann,
June 1, 1883.
Nov. 24, 1930.
"A loving wife,
A mother Dear,
Lies buried here."

MOTHER:
Martha Lynch,
Feb. 20, 1863.
Dec. 23, 1922.
"Tho lost to sight,
To Memory dear."

Rev. Orion Lynch,
Died September 30th,19--?
Aged 79 years,3 months--?

MOTHER:
Dora Lynch Wade,
June 6, 1875.
June 19, 1924.

Robert C. Wade,
June 24, 1907.
Aug. 5, 1927.
" My loving son,At rest."

FATHER:
Titus Samson-(Mason)
June 7, 1842.
May 9, 1924.
MOTHER:
Rebecca Samson,
Jan. 13, 1859.
Dec. 20, 1928.

SAMSON:

FISHER:
Martha Rebecca Fisher,
July 2, 1914.
Nov. 24, 1919.

May Sanders Fisher,
Apr. 15, 1893.
Aug. 8, 1893.

Virginia Flippen, Daughter of
Thomas J. & Amelia B. Fisher,
Born May 16, 1882.
Died July 23, 1890.

Amelia Bryan Fisher,
Nov. 12, 1850.
--------, 19--?

Thomas Jefferson Fisher,
Feb. 22, 1847.
Nov. 16, 1916.

Landa Fisher,
May 30, 1854.
Dec. 19, 1929.
" Death is eternal Life."
Why should we weep."

Martha Jane Fisher, Wife of
Wm. A. Turner,
Born July 9, 1857.
Died Oct. 23, 1932.
" Submissive to the will
of God, even unto death."

W. A. Turner,
Born Sept. 6, 1842.
Died Jan. 2, 1897.
" How desolate our home,
Bereft of thee."

To bloom in Heaven:
Orfie Lee, Dau. of
W.A. & M.J. Turner,
Born Mar. 10, 1886.
Died April 30, 1887.
Aged 1 yr. 11 mo. 20 d's.

ROBINSON:
R. R. Robinson,
1858 - 1930.

RUSSELL:
Jefferson Lee Russell,
May 1, 1869.
May 21, 1932.
His Wife, Ollie Lee Kemp,
Dec. 14, 1872.

KEMP:
Sacred to the memory of
Robt. H.,
Sept. 5, 1847.
Dec. 23, 1928.
Mary J.,
Mar. 30, 1852.
June 4, 1929.

FISHER:
James Nelson Fisher,
Jan. 30, 1878.
Sept. 16, 1924.
Willie Belle Pickering
Fisher,
Sept. 9, 1881.
Nov. 3, 1918.

FLIPPEN:
Luther B. Flippen,
1861 - 1927.
Annie McFarland Flippen,
Aug. 11, 1840.
Sept. 4, 1925.
"The Lord is my Shepherd."

DAVIS:
Joe Junior,
Sept. 4, 1913.
July 31, 1930.

WILLIAMS:
Mother:
Adelle Ford Williams,
Mar. 28, 1898.
Nov. 19, 1933.

READ:
James Seay Read,
1871 - 1920.

READ:
Sadie King,
Sept. 10, 1907.
Apr. 20, 1925.

Little Sister:
Alice T.,Daughter of
A. H. & T. B. Read,
Born July 9, 1873.
Died Mar. 20, 1875.
" We loved this tender little
one, And would have wished
her stay;But let our Father's
will be done, She shines
in endless day."

Frank Duffy Read,
9th child of
Thomas B. & Alice Read,
Nov. 11, 1888.
Feb. 12, 1919.

Maude May,Wife of
F. D. Read,
Born Mar. 8, 1889.
Died July 12, 1917.
" A loving wife,Mother dear,
Lies buried here."

Infant Son of
F. D.& M. M. Read,
Born 8,Died Sept. 27, 1916.
" Blessed are the pure in heart,
For they shall see God."

" Our Baby"
Eleanor, Dau. of
Ellen D. & T. B. Read,
Born Jan. 18, 1905.
Died Mar. 12, 1909.
"Only Asleep."

READ:
Thomas B. Read,
1867 - 1927.

Joseph Myer Read,
6th child of
Thomas B.& Alice T.Read,
Born Apr. 2, 1878.
Died Apr. 5, 1898.
Aged 20 years,3 Da.
" The Lord is my Shepherd,
I shall not want."

READ:
Thomas B. Read,
1841 - 1900.
Alice T. Read,
1847 - 1933.

Charles Smith Read,
Seventh Child of
Thos. B.& Alice T.Read,
Oct. 16, 1880.
Nov. 19, 1903.

READ:
Joe Read Pickering,
Apr. 16, 1901.
May 15, 1932.

Wm. G. Read,
1834 - 1882.

Mary Read,
1825 - 1909.

HUFFINES:
Edward Lee Huffines,
Nov. 14, 1871.
Apr. 1, 1933.

Julian Fisher,
Mar. 27, 1875.
Nov. 28, 1932.

Hugh Jordan Hodges,
Dec. 21, 1925.
July 16, 1927.
"A little bud of love,
To bloom with God above."

STONESTREET:
Carrie S. Stonestreet,
Dec. 2, 1878.
Mar. 2, 1926.
"Rest Mother,rest in quiet
sleep,While friends in
--sorrow o'er thee weep."

William Howard Petty,
Oct. 27, 1927.
July 14, 1928.
"Sleep on Sweet babe,and
take thy rest, God called
thee home,he thought it
best."

Sarah Elizabeth Wright,
Sep. 26, 1861.
MOTHER.

(Ridgewood Cemetery p.5.)

James Henry Wright,
Sept. 13, 1856.
Aug. 25, 1921.
" Gone but not forgotten."
FATHER.

Mary Elizabeth Hackett,
Sept. 22, 1899.
Oct. 14, 1931.
" Weep not,Father and Mother,
for me; For I am waiting
in Glory for thee."

HACKETT:
T. E. Jack,
Dec. 18, 1861.
June 13, 1934.
Fannie E.,His wife,
July 26, 1865.

Star Lee Farmer,
Borned Oct. 1913.
Died March 3, 1928.
" Gone but not forgotten."

J. B. Mullican,
Borned July 12, 1918.
August 28, 1931.
" Gone but not forgotten."

Samuel G. Lee,
May 5, 1849.
Jan. 30, 1916.
Matilda A. Lee,
May 27, 1852.
" Blessed are they that
die in the Lord."

Margaret Thompson Stevens,
Mar. 15, 1839.
Oct. 5, 1901.

J. T. Johnson,
1844 - 1888.

Emily A. Johnson,
1821 - 1885.

Geo. M. Key,
Sep. 27, 1832.
Jan. 12, 1916.
"An honest man,the noblest
work of God."

Florence Gardenhire Key,
Wife of Dr. R. E. Key,
May 19, 1865.
Nov. 12, 1924.

James Leslie Key,
Nov. 30, 1872.
June 10, 1935.

Abram H. King,
Aug. 17, 1850.
Feb. 16, 1933.
Sadie Duke,Wife of,
Nov. 27, 1858.

H. Grady,only daughter of
A. H. & Sadie King,
Born Aug. 10, 1889.
Died Feb. 26, 1894.

Mrs. Belle Jones,Wife of
Tom Jones,
Born Feb. 10, 1856.
Died Oct. 15, 1935.
Age 79 yrs.8 mos.5 days.
"May we cherish her memory,
and emulate her virtues."
"Gone but not forgotten."

Inft. Son of
Rev.& Mrs. J. F. Watson,
Born & Died Dec.22, 1928.

Little Jimmie Anderson,
Died like a trooper in the
office of J.J.Page Shows.
Aug. 22, 1935.

(Undertakers Marker)
Mrs.Lina Gibbs Skurlock,
Died Jan. 26, 1937.
Age 52 yrs. 7 mo.16 days.

(Ridgewood Cemetery p. 6.)

(Undertakers Marker)
Reuben Allen Angel,
Died Sept. 15, 1936.

(Undertakers Marker)
Aletha E. Conner,
May 7, 1935.
Age 67 yrs.

Dortha Mildred Ballenger,
Aug. 15, 1930.
Feb. 6, 1931.
" She was the sunshine
of our home."

(Undertakers Marker)
Mrs. Nannie Bryant,
Died Dec. 11, 1930.
Age 40 yrs.6 mo.5 days.

Tom Silcox,
Born June 15, 1898.
Mar. 25, 1936.
" Gone but not forgotten."

Little Billie Chism Butler,
Born July 7, 1932.
Died June 24, 1935.
" Gone but not forgotten."

Joy Hardcastle,
Born & Died July 22, 1936.
" Our Darling"

G. E. Hardcastle,
Died Nov. 15, 1934.
Age 65-
" Gone but not forgotten."

Melvin Silcox,
Born Oct. 25, 1905.
Died Nov. 26, 1934.
" Gone but not forgotten."

J. B. Silcox,
Born Aug. 12, 1876.
Age 54-2 mo.2D.
Died Oct. 14, 1930.
" A precious one from us
has gone,A voice we loved
is stilled;A p;ace is
vacant in our home,which
never can be filled.

Robt. Hindsley,
Died Feb. 10, 1935.
Age 65.
"Gone but not forgotten"

Nan Silcox,
Died Jan. 10, 1935.
Age 62-
"Gone but not forgotten"

I. D. Halladay,
Died Nov. 12, 1930.
Age 50 years,one month.
"Gone but not forgotten"

Ruth Evelyn Presley,
Born March 12, 1930.
Died July 24, 1934.
" Gone but not forgotten"

J. C. Mathews,
1930-

Elizabeth Rains,
Died Oct. 18, 1936.
Age 67 yrs.8 mos.26 Days.
"Gone but not forgotten"

2 Unmarked Graves.

William Jr.Goosby,
Born & Died Mar. 28,1930.
" Gone but not forgotten"

Joel Dickerson,
Died Aug. 25, 1936.
"Gone but not forgotten"

Wade S. Knight,
Jan. 8, 1896.
Nov. 28,1933.
"His toils are past,His work
is done;He fought the fight,
The victory won."

Ethel C. Stockton,
Aug. 5, 1908.
Apr. 8, 1928.

SMITH COUNTY

TOMBSTONE RECORDS

ROBINSON GRAVEYARD

This graveyard is located about 4 miles East from Defeated on a farm now owned by N. E. Robinson. Copied by Rebecca Ballenger September 2, 1936.

Susan Robinson wife of S. B. Robinson May 15, 1841 May 6, 1920
S. B. Robinson Mar. 11, 1831 April 7, 1900

TOMBSTONE - INSCRIPTIONS

SAYLE GRAVEYARD

Located on the left side of Highway No. 24, on the Lebanon
Pike, about three miles from Carthage, Tennessee. It is
about 40 feet from the Highway.
Copied by Mrs. Bessie Gibbs, and Miss Hattie Winfree, Carthage,
Tennessee.
March 31, 1937.

" Our Darling"
  Pattie Sayle,Wife of
  T. G. Bridges,
  July 1, 1882.
  June 13, 1912.
" Sleep Mother dear,
  And take thy rest;
  God called thee home,
  He thought it best."

  William Harding Sayle,
  June 13, 1861.
  Oct. 28, 1918.

  Virginia Carter Sayle,
  Aug. 20, 1860.
  June 11, 1919.
" Earth has no sorrow,
  That heaven cannot heal."

TOMBSTONE - INSCRIPTIONS

THOMPSON GRAVEYARD
SMITH COUNTY

Located 2½ miles East of Carthage, on south-side of State High-
way # 24, about 200 yards from Highway.
Old Thompson farm now owned by John Gwaltney.
Graveyard is in good condition, and has good fence.
There are about 20 unmarked graves.
Copied by Mrs. Cora Whitefield, Mrs. Bessie Gibbs, and Miss
Hattie Winfree, Carthage, Tennessee.
March 29, 1937.

THOMPSON:
V. D. Thompson,
May 11, 1834.
Sept. 6, 1916.
Mollie Thompson,
Feb. 6, 1872.
Sept. 19, 1877.
Mary Thompson, Nov. 9, 1843.
November 30, 1885.
Frank Thompson,
Nov. 1, 1885.
Oct. 2, 1886.

J. W. Thompson,
Mar. 21, 1873.
Apr. 10, 1908.

Bettie Smith, Wife of
Samuel Fitzpatrick,
1859 - 1916.
" Dear Mother, Farewell."

B. B. Thompson,
Born Oct. 13, 1850.
Died Oct. 14, 1927.

(Undertakers marker.)
Susan Melvina Thompson,
Died Dec. 30, 1934.
Age 87 years, 7 mo. 22 days.

Josie Thompson,
Born Oct. 14, 1860.
Died Feb. 2, 1926.

Martha E., wife of
G. M. Thompson,
Born June 3, 1831.
Died Jan. 22, 1906.
"Farewell, dear mother,
Sweet be thy rest."

G. M. Thompson,
Born July 22, 1829.
Died July 26, 1907.
"O! sing to thee of heaven,
My glorious Home above."

ROCK:
B.A.B.S.-1892-
D.D. 19, -1908-

ROCK:
B.E.B. 9, 1910-
D. No. 19, 1910.

TOMBSTONE - INSCRIPTIONS

TIMBERLAKE
FORD GRAVEYARD
SMITH COUNTY

ELMWOOD

Located ¼ mile from ~~Garthage~~, Tenn., on right side of
Highway No. 70, First owner, D.K. Timberlake, 2nd owner:
Rev. Mat Ford, 3rd owner: Arthur Payne, Present owner:
Mitchell Roberts. Graveyard in good condition, no fence.
(A soldier of war 1812, name unknown-)(Information obtained
from Mrs. Martha L. Craig, now living on place.)
There are 35 unmarked-and old colored graveyard below.
Copied by Miss Hattie Winfree and Mrs. Bessie Gibbs.
March 29, 1937.

Rev. D. K. Timberlake,
Born May 4, 1801.
Married to Jane Hubbard,
Dec. 9, 1823.
Died Dec. 18, 1883.
Was a preacher of Gospel
60 years.

Gone Home:
Jane Hubbard, Wife of
Rev. D.K. Timberlake,
Born Aug. 29, 1802.
Died Dec. 27, 1879.
Come on:

Susan, Wife of
Gen. A. H. Ross,
Born Mar. 24, 1810.
Died July 19, 1859.
Age 49 years, 3 months,
& 25 days.

Lean, Wife of
R. V. Brooks,
Born Mar. 6, 1843.
Died July 11, 1883.

Maggie M., wife of
C. A. Campbell,
Born Oct. 17, 1872.
Died July 18, 1891.

Grandchildren of
D.K. Timberlake:
CARDWELL;
Mary W., Daughter of
J.L. & M.G. Cardwell, — M.C. (Mary Caroline)
Born June 18, 1861.
Died July 27, 1879.
"A faithful daughter,
& sister dear;
In sweet repose,
Is sleeping here;
Her painful loss
We deeply feel,
But God can all
Our sorrows heal."

W. F. Cardwell,
Apr. 17, 1863.
Aug. 1, 1926.
"Come ye Blessed"

Lily G. Cardwell, daughter
of J.L. & M.G. Cardwell, (M.C.)
Born May 29, 1872.
Died Sept. 11, 1873.
"Sleep on sweet babe,
And take thy rest;
God called thee home,
When he thought best."

Timberlake
(Ford Graveyard p. 2.)

Maggie, daughter of
J. & M.G. Cardwell,   M.C.
Born July 21, 1876.
Died Sept. 17, 1877.
" A little bud, for earth
too fair, Is gone to
heaven to bloom there."

Cora May, dau. of
W. F. & S.V. Cardwell,
Born Jan. 9, 1897.
Died Nov. 10, 1901.
" Budded on earth to
Bloom in heaven."

Mary Frances Gibbs,
May 7, 1916.
Jan. 27, 1922.
" She was the sunshine
of our home."

FATHER:
W. H. Gibbs,
Dec. 10, 1849.
Oct. 9, 1926.
MOTHER:
Tennie Gibbs,
Jan. 10, 1858.
Jan. 14, 1936.

Daisy, wife of
M. C. Dickens,
Apr. 3, 1895.
Jan. 13, 1926.
" How Desolate our home,
Bereft of thee."

E. C. Craig,
Born May 6, 1849.
Died Feb. 4, 1915.
Martha L. Craig,
Born Mar. 25, 1857.
Died -----?
" Be ye ready, for in such
a hour as ye think not,
the son of man cometh."

TOMBSTONE - INSCRIPTIONS

VANTREASE GRAVEYARD

Located on right of Highway No. 70, from Carthage, Tenn,, in
Elmwood, about 200 yards from Highway.
Graveyard is in good condition, fenced in with rock wall.
There are 5 unmarked graves.
Copied by Mrs. Bessie Gibbs, and Miss Hattie Winfree, Carthage,
Tennessee.
March 29, 1937.

John Oliver Allgier, (Mason)
Born Oct. 8, 1831.
Died Feb. 4, 1913.
" Tho lost to sight,
To memory dear."

Martha New Allgier,
(Eastern Star)
Born June 9, 1839.
Died Jan. 23, 1909.
" We miss thee, but our
loss is thy eternal gain."

Ocie M. Allgier,
(Eastern Star)
Born Nov. 28, 1873.
Died July 3, 1900.
" How desolate our home,
Bereft of thee."

Son of J. M. &
M. M. Vantrease,
Born June 12, 1902.
Died June 13, 1902.
" How soon fades the
tender flower."

James M. Vantrease,
Oct. 30, 1856.
July 30, 1917.
"Gone Home."

Mollie Allgier,
(Eastern Star), Wife of
J. M. Vantrease,
Mar. 2, 1862.
Dec. 19, 1929.
"Farewell, dear mother,
Thy life shall ever be,
A star to guide us, to
heaven, and to thee."

Oliver Kirby, son of
S. M. & A. B. Fitzpatrick,
Born Jan. 14, ----?
Died Nov. 14, 1900.

Mary Richerson,
Feb. 17, 1902.
Feb. 19, 1934.

SMITH COUNTY

TOMBSTONE RECORDS

WEBB GRAVEYARD

This graveyard is located about 5 miles **East** from Defeated on the Old Webb Farm now owned by W. H. Cornwell. Copied by Rebecca Ballenger September 2, 1936.

Harriet R. Webb wife of Isaac Webb Nov. 18, 1795 July 14, 1862
Isaac Webb Dec. 29, 1790 Aug. 22, 1863

SMITH COUNTY

TOMBSTONE INSCRIPTIONS

WILLIAMS GRAVEYARD

Masonic Emblem

L. F. Williams
Born May 17,   1827
Died Aug. 15,   1898
 "Gone but not forgotten."

    "Farewell"
  Emily F. Williams
Born Mar. 14, 1838
Died Aug. 31, 1888
"In heaven there is one angel more."

    J. H. Williams
Born Nov. 19, 1831
Died July 27, 1905
"Tho lost to sight
To memory dear."

  Anderson Williams
  Born Jan. 30, 1819
  Died Sept. 1, 1880
"Sleep on, dear Father, and take thy
  rest in Jesus' arms forever blest."

        Pearl E. Dau. of Robt. H. and
          Ruthie B. Hailey
          Born Nov. 15, 1888
          Died Nov. 28, 1888
"A bud from earth too fair has gone to
   Heaven to blossom there."

        *   *   *

TOMBSTONE - INSCRIPTIONS

WILLIAMS GRAVEYARD
SMITH COUNTY

Located on Highway # 24, on Lebanon Pike, on right side of
road about 100 yards from road. How many miles from Carthage?
Graveyard is in fair condition, no graves without rocks.
Copied by Mrs. Bessie Gibbs, and Miss Hattie Winfree, Carthage,
Tennessee.
March 31, 1937.

J. W. Williams,
Born Feb. 29, 1860.
Died Feb. 10, 1911.
" Our fondest hopes lie
buried here, How desolate
our home, bereft of thee."

Willie Duke Williams,
Born Apr. 26, 1900.
Died May 4, 1900.

Benton Williams,
Born Nov. 17, 1879.
Died Feb. 27, 1902.
WILLIAMS.

SMITH COUNTY

TOMBSTONE - INSCRIPTIONS
WILLIAMS & WILSON GRAVEYARD

This graveyard is located in Smith County, about 7 miles from Carthage, Tennessee. Leaving Carthage cross the Cordull Hull bridge, turn to the right and travel about 7 miles. The graveyard is on a hill between the little towns of Rome and Rock City. It is about one hundred yards from the highway and can easily be seen from the highway. There are 11 unmarked graves within the graveyard fence.
Copied by Miss Mattie M. Jones, Carthage, Tennessee - Route # 2.
October 4, 1937.

Wilsye Armstead
Daughter of J.B. & Vida Williams
July 29, 1915 - August 5, 1916
"She was the sunshine of our home"

FATHER
James B. Norris
January 12, 1853
MOTHER
Betty K. Norris
September 19, 1960
March 4, 1922

John M. Marks
Born   April 30, 1848
Died   May 24, 1897
"How desolate our home
bereft of thee"

Alline Marks
Born   July 28, 1890
Died   December 26, 1892
"Budded on earth to Blossom
in Heaven"

(Masonic Emblem)
William G. Norris
Born   September 21, 1811
Died   June 2, 1881
"Dearest father thou has left us,
Here thy loss we deathly feel,
But tis God that hath bereft us,
He can all our sorrows heal"

Mary S. Norris
Born   February 1, 1827
Died   September 11, 1892
"Tho lost to sight to memory dear"

Samuel R.
Son of S. R. & V. R. Payne
Born   December 18, 1884
Died   February 10, 1885
"Too pure for earth
To heaven he has gone"

Vira R.
Daughter of
J. R. and E. Crabtree
Wife of S. R. Payne
Born   November 16, 1867
Died   December 24, 1884

W. C. Yancy
January 8, 1827 - August 18, 1885

Fannie Payne Yancy
August 20, 1843 - January 11, 1928

"Farewell"
Mary E.
Wife of W. D. Pope
Born   March 13, 1854
Died   March 14, 1884
"She was a kind and affectionate
wife,
A fond mother and a friend to all"

"In my father's house are many
mansions"
Lida B. Pope
Born   November 18, 1853
Died   June 5, 1902
"Lida we miss thee every where"

John W. Eatherly
April 20, 1847 - October 26, 1927

(Williams & Wilson Graveyard, p. 2)

Nannie Ellen Eatherly
February 18, 1850

"Gone Home"
William R.
Son of I. N. & S.A. Payne
Born   October 17, 1847
Died   January 17, 1859

J. N. Payne
Born   July 28, 1808
Died   August 13, 1894
"Be ye ready for in such an hour as
ye think not the son of man cometh"

Sally A.
Wife of Isaac N. Payne
Born   September 7, 1822
Married December 19,
Died   August 19, 1888

Louise Williams
February 22, 1885

Walter J. Williams
October 17, 1878
October 26, 1921

Horace G.
Son of A.T. and Jennie E.Williams
Born   January 30, 1905
Died   May 22, 1908
"What hopes have cherished
with you my son"

Nancy Jane
Wife of G. T. Williams
Born   May 22, 1851
Died   October 22, 1907
"We have lost our darling mother,
She has bid us all adieu,
She has gone to live in heaven
and her person is lost to view"

Geo. Wilson
Son of G. T. & N.J. Williams
Born   May 26, 1876
Died   March 16, 1889
"Our darling one has gone before
to greet us on the other shore"

Elizabeth W. Roe
Born   March 13, 1832
Died   August 20, 1867
"To pure for earth
to heaven she has gone"

Nancy
Wife of John Roe
Died (Born) December 25, 1798
Died   October 25, 1872
"Rest Mother rest in sweet sleep
while friends in sorrow o'er you
weep"

John Roe
Born   March 5, 1792
Married   December 6, 1819
Died   August 15, 1886

Willis A. Wilson
Born   March 18, 1824
Died   November 17, 1896
"An honest man the noblest work
of God"

"In my father's house are many
mansions"
N. E. Dirickson
Wife of Sylvester Dirickson
Born   April 1, 1837
Died   December 23, 1898
"In thee O Lord have I put my
trust"

Joshua T.
Son of W. A. & H. H. Wilson
Born March 25, 1847
Died   January 9, 1851
"The Angles calleth him"

Hattie O.
Daughter of W.A. & H.H. Wilson
Born   November 23, 1858
Died   June 27, 1859
"Blossomed to die"

Willis A.
Son of W. A. & H. H. Wilson
Born May 3, 1861
Died   June 13, 1861
"A Little Bird of Love"

(Williams & Wilson Graveyard, p. 3)

Sarah F.
Daughter of W. A. & H. H. Wilson
Born February 10, 1854
Died January 4, 1862
"Forever with the Lord"

Willis A. Wilson
Son of John B. & Eleanora Wilson
Born November 6, 1879
Died March 19, 1885

John B. Wilson, Jr.
Son of John B. & Eleanora Wilson
Born July 20, 1888
Died August 27, 1888
"Our babe, a tie lengthened from
earth to heaven"

Eleanora Kelley
Wife of John B. Wilson
Born January 21, 1856
Died September 29, 1909
Married at Granville Tenn.
October 31, 1876
"Stranger tread lightly on this sod
for 'neath it lies one who was my
companion for nearly 33 years and
the mother of our 8 children, may
we all meet her in heaven"

(Masonic emblem)
John B. Wilson
Born January 30, 1849
Departed this life
August 20, 1923
"Having finished life's duty
he now sweetly rests"

Willis A. Wilson
Born & Died October 31, 1910
Wilsye A. Wilson
September 10, 1919 --
October 3, 1922
Son and Daughter of
Kelly J. & Lorena Ford Wilson
"Of such is the kingdom of
heaven"

Nellie R.
Daughter of J. & A. J. Wilson
Born December 5, 1869
Died 1881
"A precious one from us has gone"

Theadore C.
Son of J. & A. J. Wilson
January 9, 1853 --
September 29, 1867

Calva D. Hatcher
March 20, 1892
March 6, 1919

TOMBSTONE - INSCRIPTIONS

WYATT GRAVEYARD
SMITH COUNTY

Located about 10 miles from Carthage, Tennessee, in Chestnut
Mound, about 50 yards from Highway # 70.
There are 20 unmarked graves. Very good condition.
Copied by Mrs. Cora Whitefield, Carthage, Tennessee.
March 29, 1937.

Johnie W. Wyatt,
Born Apr. 6, 1888.
Died June 28, 1903.
" Farewell, Sweet Johny,
Thou a star to guide into
heaven and to thee."

John F. Wyatt,
Apr. 2, 1850.
Apr. 9, 1935.
" A loving husband and
father dear; In sweet
repose is sleeping here.
His painful loss we deeply
feel; But God can all our
sorrows heal."

Mary E. Wyatt,
Born June 24, 1854.
Died Nov. 17, 1885.

Ada B. Wyatt,
Born May 28, 1883.
Died Mar. 10, 1907.
" Ada, we miss thee everywhere."

(Holy Bible)
J. G. Wyatt,
Born July 25, 1823.
Died Oct. 18, 1881.

William B. Wyatt,
Co. C. 8 Tenn.
M. T. D. Inf.

(Holy Bible)
Elritter O. Sanders,
Born Jan. 21, 1836.
Died Mar. 30, 1910.

(Elritter Sanders con't)
"Since thou can no longer
stay, To cheer me with thy
love; I hope to meet with
thee again, In yon bright
world above."

James D. Sanders,
Born Mar. 10, 1843.
Died Jan. 9, 1919.
"A loving husband, a father
dear, lies buried here."

Nettie, Wife of
W. E. Sanders,
Born March 20, 1872.
Died March 6, 1905.

William Sherman Sanders,
Died April 6th, 1936.
Aged 3 yrs. 5 mos. 18 da.

Infant son of
W. A. & A. T. Blair,
Born Aug. 24, 1905.
Died Sept. 26, 1905.

James G. Wyatt,
Born Dec. 6, 1871.
Died June 20, 1888.
Sarah A. Wyatt,
Died Oct. 20, 1896.
Aged about 63 years.
Wm. F. Wyatt,
Born Nov. 11, 1830.
Died July 5, 1901.
W. Hershal Johnson,
Born Mar. 28, 1885. Drowned
June 28, 1903. "Hershal, we
miss thee everywhere".

SMITH COUNTY

TOMBSTONE - INSCRIPTIONS

Copied by Mrs. Bessie Gibbs and Miss Hattie Winfrie, Carthage, Tennessee.

Copas (Father & Mother)
W.P.C.   O.F.C.

James A Thomas
Oct. 17, 1838
Mar. 18, 1919
"He was a good and affectionate
husband and a friend to all."

THOMAS
Eveline Thomas
July 4, 1838
Nov. 17, 1917
"She was a good and affectionate
wife and a friend to all."
Thomas

Minerva F. Yeaman
Jan 4, 1843
June 25, 1908
"Asleep in Jesus."

N. T. Yeaman
Born Dec. 11, 1834
Died Oct. 23, 1894
"An honest man is the noblest work
of God."

Oline Duke
Born Jan. 25, 1897
Died June 13, 1897
"Our fondest hopes lie buried here."

Annie dau. of
J. A. & E. Thomas
Born Oct. 14, 1866
Died Oct. 12, 1872
"Our fondest hopes lie buried here."

B. R. Son of
J. A. & E. Thomas
Born June 18, 1861
Died May 26, 1863
"Budded on earth to bloom in heaven."

Robert S. West
1883 - 1918

Ottis B. _____
Born May 22, 1894
Died Feb. 3, 1895
"Sleep on sweet babe and take thy
rest, God called thee home
He thought it best."

Masonic Emblem
H. C. Dean
Born Aug. 12, 1858
Died Oct. 10, 1901
"Gone but not forgotten."

Alice Williams Simmons
Mar. 5, 1858
Sept. 23, 1936

Polly A. West
Wife of A. Williams
Born Jan. 25, 1826
Died Mar. 27, 1909

Susan P. Williams
Born Sept. 22, 1845
Died Mar. 24, 1899
"Asleep in Jesus."

Ruthie Armistead
Apr. 8, 1884
"Her spirit smiles from that
bright shore
And softly whispers Weep no more."

R. B. Armistead
Mar. 28, 1871
Apr. 9, 1929
"Since thee can no longer stay to
cheer us with thy love
We hope to get to see thee
in that bright world above."
Mother and Father

Uncle
Walter J Smith
Aug. 9, 1880
Oct. 2, 1922
"Be ye ready, for ye know
not the hour the Son of Man
cometh."

Brother
Bedford Richardson
June 29, 1891
Aug. 4, 1923
"An honest man the noblest work
of God."

Willie Roberta Smith
Oct. 11, 1911
Apr. 3, 1926
"Weep not Father and Mother for me
For I am waiting in glory for
thee."

Mary Jane Smith
Oct. 30, 1924
Feb.   7, 1936
"A little flower of love."

Allie Mai Smith Davis
Nov. 26, 1907
Oct. 18, 1934
"Gone but not forgotten."

Stella Anderson
Born Feb. 22, 1888
Died Apr. 4, 1935
"Gone but not forgotten."

Nannie Mai Durham
Born Sept. 23, 1906
Died Feb. 14, 1928
"Gone but not forgotten."

Hugh B. Williams
1895 - 1931

Infant of S. L. & S. E. Anderson
Born Nov. 20, 1928
Died Mar. 20, 1929
"Asleep with Jesus."

Infant of S. L. & S. E. Anderson
June 20, 1926
"Asleep with Jesus."

Infant of S. L. & S. E. Anderson
Jan. 20, 1927
"Asleep with Jesus."

M. W. A. Emblem

Larkie A. Russell
Feb. 22, 1869
Jan. 24, 1916
"A precious one from us is gone,
A voice we loved is stilled
A place is vacant in our home
Which never can be filled."

Alethia J. Russell
June 6, 1850
Dec. 22,1932
In Memory of Mother
"God in his wisdom has recalled
the boon his love had given
And though the body slumbers here
the soul is safe in heaven."

"Come Ye Blessed"
Wm. Russell
May 30, 1846
May 15, 1921
"Since thou canst no longer stay
and cheer us with thy love,
We hope that we will meet again
in that bright world above."

*   *   *   *

TENNESSEE

RECORDS OF SMITH COUNTY

CHURCH MINUTES 1866
ROUND LICK BAPTIST ASSOCIATION
BILDAD MEETING HOUSE

HISTORICAL RECORDS PROJECT
Official Project No. 165-44-3-115

COPIED UNDER WORK'S PROGRESS ADMINISTRATION

MRS. JOHN TROTWOOD MOORE
STATE LIBRARIAN & ARCHIVIST, SPONSOR

MRS. ELIZABETH D. COPPEDGE
DIRECTOR OF WOMEN'S & PROFESSIONAL PROJECTS

MRS. PENELOPE JOHNSON ALLEN
STATE SUPERVISOR

MISS MATILDA A. PORTER
SUPERVISOR SECOND DISTRICT

COPIED BY
MISS BESSIE GIBBS

TYPED BY
MISS HUGH CATHEY
MISS LUCILLE WOOD

June 6, 1938

SMITH COUNTY

CHURCH MINUTES

NEW INDEX
1866

THIRTIETH ANNUAL
ROUND LICK BAPTIST ASSOCIATION.

A

Agee, W. D. 2,

B

Barbee, J., 2,
Bass, S., 2,3,4,
Bean, S., 3,
Bellar, J., 2,
Bildad, 2,
Bildad Meeting House, 1,
Brush Creek, 2,

C

Cumberland, 2,3,

D

Deadman, J., 3,
Dekalb County, 4,
Dodd, J., 2,

E

Earp, J., 3,
Elk River, 2,3,
Enon, 2,
Evans, S.F. 2,3,4,

F

Fain, R. W. 3,
Filips, J., 2,
Fitzpatrick, S., 2,3,
Franklin, Tennessee, 1,
Frost, P.E. 2,3,

G

H

Helton Creek, 2,4,
Hick Creek, 2,

I

J

Johnson, D., 2,

K

King, J., 2,3,

L

Lancaster, P.M.2,3,4,

M

Magness, P.G. 2,3,4,
Mofitt, G. P. 2,
Mt. Pleasant, 2,

N

Newbell, T. W. 2,3,
Night, J. A. 2,

O

Owen, E. D. 2,
Owen, W. B. 2,

P

Petty, J., 2,3,4,
Potter, W. 2,3,

R

Raglin, J. C. 2,
Roark, W. S. 2,
Round, Lick, 1,2,

S

Salt Lick, 2,
Sequatchee, 3,
Sinking Cre'k, 2, 4,
Smart, J. A. 2,3,4,
Stone's River, 2,3,

T

Tennessee, 4,
Testament, 2,

U

V

W

Wagoner, J. 2,3,
Walker, H. J. 2,3,
West, C.W. 2,3,
West, M. F. 2,4,
Wiliby, J., 2,
Wood, C., 3,
Wright, S. H. 2,3,4,

Y

Yeargan, D., 2,3,4,

SMITH COUNTY

CHURCH MINUTES 1866
ROUND LICK BAPTIST ASSOCIATION
BILDAD MEETING HOUSE

This record is owned at present by Edd Agee, Gordonsville, Tennessee, Star Route.

Copied by Bessie Gibbs, Carthage, Tennessee, Route # 2 - July 1937.

* * * * * *

The Thirtieth Annual Round Lick Baptist Association Began and Held with the Church at Bildad Meeting House, on Saturday before the First Lord's day in September, 1866 and two days following.
(Weekly Review Print, Franklin, Tenn.) - 1866.
(p 2)   Minutes.
A discourse, introductory to business was delivered by Elder P. G. Magness, from the 6th. chapter and 45th. verse of John: "It is written in the prophets and they shall be all taught of God," &C.

CHURCHES	MESSENGERS	No. Meetings	Baptized	Received by Letter	Dismissed by Letter	Excluded	Restored	Dead	Members	Contributions $	For Deficiency	For A Book
Salt Lick	J.Petty*, C.W. West, J.A. Night	1	20		1	2		4	71	3	50	50
Round Lick	S.Bass*, J.Barbee, J.Filips	1							59	3	60	50
Mt. Pleasant	L.F.Evans*, S.Fitzpatrick, J. Bellar	4	2		1	1			36	2	50	50
Testament	M.F. West*, W.S. Roark, J.C. Raglin	2	2					5	38		50	50
Hick Creek	G. W. Newbell, W. D. Agee	2		1				1	47	3	1	50
Enon	No Intelligence											
Bilad	P.G. Magness*, J.Dodd, W.Potter	2	16			1		2	100	2	50	50
Helton Creek	D.Yeargan, D.Johnson*, J.Wiliby	1	6						17	1		50
Brush Creek	P.M.Lancaster*, S.H.Wright*, J.A. Smart*	3	1			3	7		47	3		50

Sinking Crik - No Intelligence

* Ordained

The Association then organized by choosing Elder P. M. Lancaster Moderator.

Invitation was given for the reception of Churches. None came forward.

Corresponding letters were called for in the following order: From Stone's River - Letter and Minutes, by her messengers, W. B. Owen and E. D. Owen. Cumberland no Letter, but minutes, by her messengers, Elder J. King and Brother H. J. Walker. Elk River - no Letter, but minutes, by her messengers, Elders P. E. Frost, G. P. Moffit, J. Wag - (p-3) oner, and Brothers C. Wood and J. Earp S _____ (?) Letter and minutes by her messengers, Elder G. W__ker (Walker?) and S. Bean.

The corresponding brethern were invited to seats, visiting brethern were invited to seats also.

The Association then appointed Elders P. G. Magness, S. H. Wright, S. Bass, J. Petty and Bro. S. Fitzpatrick with the Moderator and Clerk a committee to arrange the business of the Association and report when called on. Then appointed C. W. West and G. W. Newbell, a Committee of Finance, to report when called upon.

Appointed Elders R. W. Fain, G. W. Walker and J. E. Frost to occupy the stand on tomorrow, Sunday, and that Divine Service begin at 10 o'clock A.M. After praise and prayer by Elder G. Walker, adjourned until 9 o'clock Monday morning.

On Sunday, the Brethern agreeable to appointment, preached the word to a large and attentive Audience, and, we hope, to Divine acceptance.

Monday Morning, 9 o'Clock. - met pursuant to adjournment, praise and prayer by Elder J. E. Frost.

The roll of messengers called, a quorum being present, and the Rules of Decorum being read, the Association proceeded to business in the following order:

1st. The Committee to whom the arrangements were referred was called, who reported and were discharged.

2nd. Requested Elders J. King, S. Bean and J. Waggoner to preach today, Monday.

3rd. Called for letters of correspondence to sister Associations with whom we correspond, which were handed in by the Clerk, who was appointed to write them, and disposed of in the following manner:

To Stone's River - by Elders S. Bass, J. Bass, J. Petty and L. F. Evans.

To Cumberland - by Elders J. Petty, L. F. Evans and Brethern D. Yeargan and J. Deadman.

To Elk River - Elders P. G. Magness, P. M. Lancaster and Brother W. Potter.

To Sequachee - Elders M. F. West, J. Petty, J. A. Smart, P. G. Magness, and Brothers S. Fitzpatrick and C. W. West, (p 4) 4th. call on the Committee of Finance, who reported the contribution to be $20. for the use of the Association for the deficincy $375 and $410 to buy a book

5. Appointed Elder S. Bass to preach our next introductory sermon and in case of failure, Elder J. Petty, his alternate.

6. Appointed the Clerk to superintend the printing of the minutes and to have 400 copies printed and distributed the same, and be allowed the remainder for his services.

7. The next Association to be held with the Church at Helton Creek

85

(Round Lick Baptist Association, p. 3)

Meeting House, Dekalb county, Tennessee, commencing on Saturday before the first Lord's day in September, 1867. Divine Service to commence at 10 o'clock A. M.

8. Appointed L. F. Evans to purchase a book, and P. M. Lancaster to transcribe the minutes of our Association in it and have $10 for his services, and request the churches to contribute to pay the same.

9. Recommend the brethern in the Ministry to attend the church at Sinking Creek, the next year, in the following order: First Saturday and Sunday before November, Eld's. P. G. Magness and D. Yeargan; December, P. M. Lancaster and S. H. Wright; January and February, P. G. Magness; March J. Petty and M. F. West; April, J. A. Smart and P. G. Magness; May, L. F. Evans and S. Bass, June; P. M. Lancaster and D. Yeargan; July, S. H.Wright and J. A. Smart; August, J. Petty and M. F. West.

10th. Appointed Elders S. Bass and P. M. Lancaster, a committee, to inquire into the non-representation of Enon.

There being no further business, the Association, after praise and prayer by Elder S. Bass, adjourned to meet at the time and place above mentioned.

P. M. Lancaster Moderator
L. F. Evans Clerk

End.

TENNESSEE

RECORDS OF SMITH COUNTY

CHURCH MINUTES
1799-1807

HISTORICAL RECORDS PROJECT
OFFICIAL PROJECT NO. 465-44-3-115

COPIED UNDER WORKS PROGRESS ADMINISTRATION

MRS. JOHN TROTWOOD MOORE
STATE LIBRARIAN & ARCHIVIST, SPONSOR

ELIZABETH D. COPPEDGE
STATE DIRECTOR OF WOMEN'S & PROFESSIONAL PROJECTS

PENELOPE JOHNSON ALLEN
STATE SUPERVISOR

CAROLINE SMALL KELSO
SUPERVISOR

HATTIE FERRELL WINFREE
COPYIST

MAY MANNING
TYPIST

MARCH 24, 1938

blank

SMITH COUNTY

CHURCH MINUTES
1799 - 1807

NEW INDEX.

<table>
<tr><td colspan="2">A</td><td>Page</td><td></td><td>Page</td></tr>
<tr><td>Abram, (Negro)</td><td></td><td>41</td><td>Burford, Bro. Daniel</td><td>1,5,6,11
12,20,40</td></tr>
<tr><td>Agness, (Negro)</td><td></td><td>2,6</td><td>Burfords, Bro.</td><td>4,18,19</td></tr>
<tr><td>Allen, Bro.</td><td></td><td>26</td><td colspan="2" style="text-align:center">C</td></tr>
<tr><td>Allen, Capt. Grant</td><td></td><td>1,5,11,12,15
16,17,18,20</td><td>Cany Fork</td><td>27,32,39,41</td></tr>
<tr><td>Allen, Clifton</td><td></td><td>5,10,11</td><td>Chandler, Elizabeth</td><td>41</td></tr>
<tr><td>Allen's Meeting House</td><td></td><td>31,49,50</td><td>Charles, (Negro)</td><td>2,3,6,11</td></tr>
<tr><td colspan="2" style="text-align:center">B</td><td></td><td>Churches:
  Baptist
  Whites Creek</td><td>54
20,21,36</td></tr>
<tr><td>Banks, Bro.</td><td></td><td>15,16</td><td></td><td></td></tr>
<tr><td>Banks, Kirinch</td><td></td><td>6,11</td><td>Creeks:
  Dixon
  Goose</td><td>1,5,7,54
23</td></tr>
<tr><td>Banks, Q.</td><td></td><td>52</td><td></td><td></td></tr>
<tr><td>Banks, Rich'd</td><td></td><td>1,6,11</td><td colspan="2" style="text-align:center">D</td></tr>
<tr><td>Banks, Sister</td><td></td><td>1</td><td>Dixon's Creek</td><td>1,5,7,54</td></tr>
<tr><td>Banks, Thomas</td><td></td><td>32,34,38,49,51</td><td>Dixon's Creek Meeting House</td><td>21</td></tr>
<tr><td>Baptist Church</td><td></td><td>54</td><td>Dorris, Bro. Joseph</td><td>20,21,22,26</td></tr>
<tr><td>Barton, Benj.</td><td></td><td>6,11,34,49</td><td>Dorrises Meeting House</td><td>20,22</td></tr>
<tr><td>Bolton, Charles</td><td></td><td>29</td><td>Doughty, M.</td><td>6</td></tr>
<tr><td>Bolton, Elizabeth</td><td></td><td>29</td><td>Doughty, Mary</td><td>23</td></tr>
<tr><td>Britain, Bro.</td><td></td><td>14</td><td>Doughty, Saml.</td><td>6,23</td></tr>
<tr><td>Britain, Nelly</td><td></td><td>6</td><td style="text-align:center">E (No E's)</td><td></td></tr>
<tr><td>Britain, P.</td><td></td><td>6</td><td style="text-align:center">F</td><td></td></tr>
<tr><td>Britain, Peggy</td><td></td><td>26</td><td>Ford, Edmond</td><td>51</td></tr>
<tr><td>Britain, Bro. Rich'd</td><td></td><td>6,11,13,23</td><td>Frank, (Negro)</td><td>29</td></tr>
</table>

Smith Church Minutes
New Index   p. 4 blank

(92)

SMITH COUNTY

CHURCH MINUTES
1799 - 1807.

P-1.   Saturday before (the) second Lords day in 1799-

A Conference of the Members of Bro. Phipps (?) Church living in the (town)
of Dixon Creek, (torn off) Capt. G. Allen, (torn off)

No business of importance brought before (the Church.
        Appointed the Lord's Supper to be Administered at next Meeting
            in Course.
        Bro. William Martin appointed Deacon --
        Bro. R. Banks & Sister Banks recd by Letter
        Bro. Danl. Burford recd by Letter
P-2.   (Sister) Agness a black Woman (And Bro. Charles a black man
            recd by Experience --
        Next Meeting to be at the same place, on the Saturday before
            the Second Lords day in Next month --

        Saturday before the Second Lords day in Novr.

the members met, Mr. Wm. McGee, preached from these Words, There are three
things which agree on earth, the spirit, the Water and the Blood

P-3.   recd Bro. Benj. Johns by Letter, - &
        Bro. Charles Baptized,

        Saturday before the Second Sunday in Decr.

the Members met at the same place, but nothing done of Consequence.

        Appointed the next Church Meeting to be in March or Sooner if
            found Requisite --

        Saturday before the first Lords day in Jany 1800

A church Meeting being Called to look into the Conduct of Bro. John Hall, the
Members Met agreeable to appointment and after prayer proceeded to business.

P-4.   After Charges of Bro. Hall, being investigated he Was found guil-
            ty of Charging Harberd Lenear Hireling exorbitantly for work
            done for him, to the amount of Two Dollars, Which Money Bro.
            Hall promises to refund to sd Hiriling - the Church Waits With
            Bro. Hall till the Saturday before the Second Lords day in

P-4.   Febry for him to report his repentance,

            Saturday before the second Lords day in Feby.

the Church Met in Conference at Bro. Burfords,

Bro. Hall reports to the Church that he had seen the impropriety of his
        Conduct towards   (P-5)   the sd Hirilings, from which he was
        restored to full fellowship

            Saturday before the second Lords day in March

the Church Met at Capt. Allens.

Isaac Toadvine, William Phipps, Joshua White, And Clifton Allen Also at-
        tended, they being appointed as a presbytery to Ordain Daniel
        Burford to Ministry of the Gospel, Which accordingly Was done.
        They also Constituted the Arm of Bro. Phipps Church, being on Dix-
        ons Creek into a district Church Consisting of the Members whose
        names are as Followeth (Viz)

P-6. Male - March 8th 1800		Females	
Danl Burford	1	K. Banks	1
Rd Britain	2	S. Hall	2
Wm. Martin	3	M. Stalkup	3
Rd Banks	4	F. Martin	4
Benj. Barton	5	S. Mabis	5
Thos. Lacy	6	M. Hammock	6
Thos. Stubblefield	7	Nelly Britain	7
Benj. Johns	8	Sarah ◊ Black	8
John Hall	9	Rose ◊ do	9
Tom ◊ Black	10	Agnes ◊ do	10
Charles ◊ do	11	D. Sitton	11
Apr. 2		M. Sitton	12
Jas. Sitton	12	S. Shrum	13
Jeffrey Sitton	13	Priss ◊ Black Woman	14
Mar. 1801		M Johnston	15
Saml. Hires	14	M. Daughty	16
Jacob Kenedy	15	P. Britain	17
Apr. 11		17 Male	
John Johnston	16	17 F. Male	
Saml. Daughty	17	34 Whole No.	

P-7.   We the Members of the Church of Jesus Christ, on Dixons Creek, in
            Smith County and parts adjaunt in the State of Tennessee, Holding
            & believing the fall of mankind into a State of Condemnation by
            the Transgression of the first Adam And the degeneracy of their
            Nature in Consequence of their legal Union to him as their head
            and representative Father, that in this their Natural State, they
            are not able to Will or do what is pleasing to God, but as he

P-7.   Woarks in them by his Spirit,   (P-8)   That Jesus Christ the Second Adam Covenanted With his father to take the seed of Abraham into a personal Union With the divine nature, And there in obey the precepts and suffer the penalty of the divine law to Make an Atonement for Sins, and bring in an everlasting Righteousness for the justification ofcall that Shall believe on him, - that the father gave him a Seed as recompence for his Humiliation, and that they Were Chosen in him as a Representative head before the foundation of the World, that in time they are (P-9)   effectually Called to repentance and faith in Christ Jesus, Sanctifyed by his spirit and kept by his power, through faith unto eternal salvation,   That such persons are intitled to and aught to be Baptized by Immersion in the name of the Father, Son, and Holy Ghost,   that Jesus Christ Will come in the last day to judge the World, and there shall be a Resurrection of the body both of the just and unjust, and the righteous shall be recieved into life eternal, and that the Wicked sent into everlasting punishment, and that the Chaeaters entering into those different   (P-10)   States shall Continuethe subjects of them eternally those We profess to believe so fare as we understand them,--and in Consiquence of the Unity of our Sentiments, - Having given ourselves to the Lord, do now in the presence of God and our Brethren, William Phipps, Isaac Toadvine, Joshua White, And Clifton Allen, Presbytery, Chosen And Called as Witnesses, give ourselves to each other by the Will of god,--to Walk in his Statues and Ordinances, to Maintain A gospel decipline among ourselves to Attend duly thereunto and to discharge   (P-11) All those Relatives duties of Watchingover, Reproving, Rebuking, Exorting and Admonishing each other, in love, as fare as god Will enable us, in Testimony Whereof, We Hereunto Subscribed our Names at the House of Capt. Grant Allens, this 8th day of March Annodom 1800

Witnesses	Isaac Toadvine	◊	Rd Britain
	Wm. Phipps	◊	Benj. Barton
	Josha White	◊	Kirinch Banks
	Clifton Allen	◊	Seeah (?) Hall
	Danl Burford	◊	Tom) Black
	Richd Banks	◊	Charles) do
	Wm. Martin	◊	Sarah) do
	Presbytery	◊	Rose) do

P-12.

      Saturday before the Second Lords Day in April

the Church Met in Conference at Capt. Allens And Siting in Order,   Appointed Bro. Danl. Burford Moderator.   The Church Resolves that All decisions in the Church Touching   Fellowship shall be by the unanimous Voice of the Church,   Queare, Whether or Not a Member shall be Called to an Account before the Church, for a publick Transesession Without being privately dealt With.

        Ansr.   they shall or May

P-13.

Queare, is it Consistent With a <u>Christin</u> Conduct to lend or hire a Horse to be run in a Race,

Ansr. No.

The Church being Informed that Bro. Richd Britain had hired or <u>lent</u> his mare to run in a Course race, We think proper to Cite him to the nextChurch Conference in Course, Which is to be at Wm. Martins, the Saturday before the second Lords day in May

P-14.   Bro. Wm. Martin & Bro. Lacy appointed to Cite Bro. Britain to Attend.

Queare, is it disorder in a <u>M</u>ember not to take a <u>S</u>eat at a Communion.

Ansr. it is

Saturday before the Second Lords day in May

Met in Conference at Bro. Wm. Martins & after <u>divine</u> <u>Survice</u> proceeded to the Case of Bro. Britain.

                         he repents, and <u>sis</u> (says) he has seen the <u>I</u>mpropriety of his
                         <u>C</u>onduct, for <u>W</u>hich Acknow<u>ledgmt</u> he was Restored to Fellowship
P-15.   Jeffrey Sitton recd by letter
                         The Administration of the Lords Supper Appointed to be the sec-
                         ond Sunday in June at Capt Allens,
                         Pris, Black Woman rec'd by <u>L</u>etter

Saturday before the second Sunday in June

the Church met in <u>C</u>onfference At Capt. Allens,

        Appointed Bro. Wm. Martin Bro. Johns & Bro. Banks to View three
          Certain (P-16)   places in Nomination for the purpose of
          buildinga Meeting House & report to the Situation of sd
          places.
        John Hall & his Wife Susannah Hall dismissed by Letter.

Saturday Before the Second Sunday in July,

the Church Met in Conference at Capt. Allens,

        Bro. Martin Bro. Banks And Bro. Johns, reports to the Church
        the <u>S</u>ituation of the af<u>oresd</u> <u>M</u>entioned places in <u>N</u>omination for
        Building a Meeting house (P-17)   It being put to <u>V</u>oat appears

P-17.   that the Meeting house shall be built at or Near Capt Grant Allens.

The Clerk directed by the Church to Write letters to those Gentle-
men, Who proposed to let them have a Situation for building said
Meeting House, on returning them thanks for there Kind offers,

Queare, shall a Member remain in fellowship With the Church
Who (P-18) joins himself to the free Masons Society or
one that has been a Mason previous to his being a Member of
the Church Who Shall at any time associate With them at their
Lodges or Meeting for the purpose of doing business With
them

Answered in the Negative

Saturday before the Second Lords day in August

Met in Conferrence at Capt. Allens

Appointed Bro. Burford & Bro. Johns Deligates to the associa-
tion.
P-19.   The Clerk directed to Write a letter to the Association With the
Assistance of Bro. Burford.

Saturday before the Second Lords day in Sepr.

met in Conferrence at the usial place

the letter to Association, read, Approved of, And assigned by the
Clerk in the behalf of the Whole Church

Saturday before the Second Lords day in October

met in Conferrence at the usial place.

pursuant to a request of the Association that (P-20) A Member
from each Church should attend at Bro. Dorrises Meeting House to
Investigate Certain Charges Against Bro. Dorris and his Church
laid in by by Whites Creek Church, We appoint Bro. Danl. Burford.

Saturday before the Second Lords day in Feby.

Met in Conference at Capt. Allens, read Certain Charges addressed
by Whites Creek Church Against Joseph Dorris and his Church,

Agreed to defer a disission on it until next conferrence in Course,

P-21.   Saturday Before the Second Lords day in March,

Met in Conference at Dixons Creek Meeting House, -

> Recd Saml Hires & Jacob Kennedy by Letter
> And having investigated the Charges exhibited against Bro. Joseph
>   Dorris, the Church to Which he belongs (by Whites Creek Church)
>   Together With the reply of the sd. Bro. Dorris And Church to
>   the same, all of Which is Contained in reports of a presby-
>   tery Who sat on the occasion at   (P-22)   Dorrises Meeting
>   House Novr. 10th 1800 pursuant to recoomendation of the last
>   Association,--
> We are of An opinion that the Charges Against the Church and
>   paster, Were Not sufficently Supported so as to Criminate
>   either Dorris or sd Church, yet we think that some expres-
>   sions used by Bro. Dorris in his reply to the last charge
>   Against him (Viz) that he expected it Was the Intention of
>   the Association to expell him and the sd. Church from the
>   General Union that Some part of their   (P-23)   Conduct
>   had painted it out, that if they did so they Would have a
>   Refuge here - is unguarded and harsh and for Which he aught
>   to Make Satisfactory Acknowledgments.
> Recd Bro. John Johnston And Sister Mary Johnston his Wife by
>   Letter

        Saturday before the fourth Lords day in Apr.

Met in Conference at Bro. Richd Britains on Goose Creek,

        And there recd by letter Saml Doughty & Mary Doughty his Wife

(Pages 24 and 25 blank)

P-26.   and Peggy Britain by Letter.

        Saturday before the Second Lords day in May 1801.

The Church Met in Conferrence,

Bro. Allen preached, Then the Church proceeded to the business of the day,

        Considered the papers lodged With us Vs. Bro. Jos. Dorris from
        Whites Creek Church & are of an opinion that the Matter therein
        Contained is also Contained in the report of a Committee appoint-
        ed Pursuant to the advice of the Association to Investigate the
        Course of   (P-27)   utterly prohibiting any of their body at-
        tending the Masonic Society in any Case Whatever

        Saturday before the 1st Sunday in August

Met in conference Agreeable to order of the Church at the Mouth of Cany
Fork,

P-27. After Divine Survice, proceeded to the business of the day

P-28. Recd Willis Hodges on the Credit of a letter into our fellowship,
            Which is to be returned to his Wife.
        Recd. James Killebrew & his Wife Nancy Killebrew by letter
            into our fellowship,
        Recd. Hicker Killebrew And Martha Killebrew on the Credit of a
            letter into our fellowship Which is to be returned to Thos.
            Killebrew

P-29. Recd Jacob Halk & Polly Halk by letter into our fellowship.
        Recd Charles Bolton & his Wife Elizabeth Bolton by letter into
            our fellowship
        Recd Stephen (Black Man) by letter into our fellowship
        Rec'd Frank (Black Man) by letter into our fellowship
        Recd Nancy Pasmore by letter into our fellowship.

P-30. Recd Temperance Smith by letter into our fellowship
        Recd Ann Morris by letter into our fellowship
        Recd Patt (Black Woman) by experience into our fellowship

P-31. Recd Joe (Black Man) by experience into our Fellowship, and
            Baptized the same that is Patt & Joe, the day Following

            Saturday before the 2nd Lords day in Augt.

Met in Conference at Allens Meeting house.after divine Survice Proceed
to Church Business

P-32. Brethren Wm. Martin   Jas. Sitton
        Miles West   Benjn Johns
        Alexander Piper and   Thomas Banks

        appointed to attend at the Mouth of the Cany Fork the Saturday
        before the First Sunday in September next to set in Conference
        With the Brethren of that Vicinity, (P-33) And report to the
        Church &c.

        Brethren Miles West Wm. Martin & Joseph Sitton Appointed as del-
        egates to the next Association to Commence the Saturday before the
        4th Sunday in September next And invested with power to Act as
        they shall think proper in behalf of the Church.

P-34. Brethren William Martin and Thomas Banks appointed to Write a
        letter to the Association

        Order that the Treasurer Bro. Benj. Barton Furnish the delegates
        With Six dollars to bare them expence to & from the association
        and also to pay Br. Miles West (P-35) one dollar pr day to
        Indemnify him for his trouble going to and from the association.

        Ordered that the Treasurer Furnish the delegates With Two dollars
        to pay for the Minutes of the Association

P-36. Queare, What measures would be proper to be pursued, With a Mem-
        ber of our Society, Who attends a Franasion Lodge, or Lodges either

P-36.   for the purpose of doing business With them or otherwise,

         Answer,   deal With them as other Transgressors.

         Wm. Norman & his Wife Betsy Norman dismissed by letter.

P-37.   The Whole number in Fellowship returned to the association Sept.
         1806, is 76, if no mistake.

              Saturday Before the 2nd Lords day in September

Met in Conference at Allens Meeting house

After prayer proceeded to Church Business

         Br. George Tilman dismissed by Letter.
         The Brethren in the Vicinity of Carthage Are Constituted an arm
            of this Church.

         Ordered that the Clerk Br. Thomas Banks Furnish the Brethren afore-
         said With a Coppy of all the proceedings of the Church Meeting
         Holden at the Mouth   (P-39)   of the Cany Fork the Saturday Be-
         fore the first Lords day in August last past.

         Also a Coppy of the articles of our faith and order, and deliver
         the same, that is the aforesd Coppies, to the aforesd Brethren
         on the Saturday before the 1st Sunday in October next.

P-40.   Br. Thomas Stubblefield Appointed a Messenger to the association
         in the room of Br. William Martin

              Saturday before 1st Sunday in Sept. 1806

Met in Conference at the Mouth of the Cany Fork.

After divine Survice proceeded to the business of the day,

         Br. Danl. Barton Chosen Moderator
         Br. Benjn Johns appointed Clerk, -
         Recd Jonas Whitley by letter into our fellowship
         Recd Deliah Stallings by letter into our fellowship
P-41.   Recd Willis Hodges & his Wife Lucy by letter into our Fellowship,
         Recd Elizabeth Chandler by by letter into our Fellowship
         Recd Kitchen, Thomas, & Martha Killibrew by letter into our Fellow-
            ship.
         Recd Abram & William (Black Men both) Belonging to Col. William
            Walton by Experience and Baptized the same, The Meeting to
            be held at the Mouth of the Cany Fork the Saturday before the
            1st Sunday in every Month, Benjn Johns, Clk.

P-42.   The Following Scriptures Aludes to Church Decipline &c.

Leviticus 13:1.2.3.4.5.6.7.8

1. And the lord spake unto Moses and Aaron, saying,
2. When a man shall have in the skin of his flesh arising a acab or bright spot, and it be in the skin of his flesh like the plague of Lebrosy then he shall be brought unto Aaron the priest, or unto one of his sons the priests,
3. And the priest shall look on the plague in the skin of the flesh, & when the hair in the plague is turned White, and the plague in sight be deeper then the skin of his flesh, it is a plague of Leprosy and the priest shall look on him, And pronounce him unclean

P-43.

4. If the bright spot be White in the skin of his flesh, and in sight be not deeper than the skin and the hair thereof be not turned white, then the priest shall shut up him that hath the plague seven days
5. and the priest shall look on him the seventh day, and, behold, if the plague in his sight be at a stay, and the plague Spread not in the skin then the priest shall shut him up seven days more
6. and the priest shall look on him again the seventh day and behold if the plague be somewhat dark and the plague spread not in the skin the priest shall pronounce him Clean. It is but a scab and he shall wash his Clothes and be Clean.
7. But if the scab is much Abroad in the skin, after that he hath been seen of the priest for his Cleansing he shall be seen of the priest Again
8. And if the priest see, that behold, the scab spreadeth in the skin, then the priest shall pronounce him unclean; it is a Leprosy

P-44.

Matthew 18th; 15,16,17

15th. Moreover if thy Bro shall trespass Against the, go and tell him his fault between thee him Alone, if he shall hear thee thou hast gained thy Bro.
16th. But if he Will not hear thee, then take With thee one or two more, that in the Mouth of two or three Witnesses, every Word may established,
17th. And if he shall neglect to hear them, tell it unto the Church, but if he neglect to hear the Church, let him be unto thee as an heathen man and a publican.

I Cor. 5:4-5

4th. in the name of the lord Jesus Christ When ye are gathered together, And my spirit, With the power of the lord Jesus Christ,
5th- to diliver such an one unto satain for the distreection of the flesh, that the spirit may be saved in the day of the lord Jesus.

P-45.

I Cor. 8:9-10-11-12-13

9th. but take heed, least by any Means this liberty of yours become a stumbling block to them that are Weak,
10 For if any Man see thee Which hast knowledge set at meat in the idols temple, shall not the Confession of him Which is Weak be emboldened to eat those things Which are of-

P-45.   fered to Idols,
        11th. Through thy knowledge shall the Weak Bro. Perish for Whom
              Christ died
        12th. But When ye sin so Against the Brethren, and Wound their Weak
              Conscience, ye sin Against Christ.
        13th. Wherefore, if Meat Make my Bro. to offend I Will eat no flesh
              While the World standeth, lest I make my Bro. to offend

P-46.   2 Cor. 2:4,5,6,7th
        7th so that Contray Wise, ye aught rather to forgive him, and
             Comfort him, lest perhaps such a one should be swallowed
             up, With over much sorrow

                               Gal. 6:1-2
        1.   Brethren if a Man be overtaken in a fault, ye Which are spir-
             itual restore such an one in the spirit of Weakness, Con-
             sidering thy self, lest thou also be tempted,
        2.   Bear ye one anothers burdens, & so fulfil the law of Christ

             Saturday before the 4th Lords day in October 1806

Met in Conference at Martins Meeting house

(Pages 47 & 48 torn out)

P-49. After prayer, proceeded to Church business

        Brethren Benjamin Barton & Thos Banks Appointed to Write to the
        Brethren to attend next Meeting in Course at Allens Meeting house
        As there is business of importance to look into

        Br. Miles West requested to preach to us statedly. He Bro. West
        ses he is Willing if the Lord permits.

P-50.   Saturday before the 2nd Lords day in Novemr.

Met in Conference at Allens Meeting house,

After prayer, proceeded to Church Business After the usual Manner--

        Bro. Miles West Chosen Moderator,
        Church Meeting to be only once a Month at Allens Meeting house,

            Saturday before the 2nd Sunday in Decr.

Met in Conferrence at Allens Meeting house.

After prayer proceeded to business

P-51.   Ordered that Brother Joseph Sitton be Allowed $5 for going to the
         Church on Mnday to Settle A grivance

         Recd Isaac (Black Man) & Mary (Black Woman) by Experiance belong-
         to Edmond Ford. For further particulars Refer to the other book.
         Thos. Banks Clk.

P-52.   There Was 100 Members in fellowship returned to the last associa-
         tion Sept. 1807. T. Banks Clk.

P-53.   (blank)

P-54.   (Form) Baptist Church on Dixons Creek, Smith County, State of Ten-
         nessee, Holding believers baptism by Immersion, the doctrine of
         particular Election, effectual Calling, and the final persirvance
         of the Saints, Hath hereby dismissed our Brother A. in full fellow-
         ship When Joined to any other Church of the same faith & Order.
               Signed by order of the Church

                                        By   Wm Martin
                                             1st Deacon

                          THE END

INDEX

INDEX

INDEX

INDEX

INDEX

WILLIAMS, Polly A. West, 77
WILLIAMS, R. C., 29
WILLIAMS, Sarah, 1
WILLIAMS, Susan P., 77
WILLIAMS, Thomas, 39
WILLIAMS, Vida, 73
WILLIAMS, W. T., 40
WILLIAMS, Walter J., 74
WILLIAMS, Willie Duke, 72
WILLIAMS, Wilsye Armstead, 73
WILLIAMS, Wm.? K., 50
WILLIAMSON, Sallie A., 55
WILLIFORD, J. M., 59
WILSON, A. J., 75
WILSON, Cornelia, 27
WILSON, Eleanora, 75
WILSON, Eleanora Kelley, 75
WILSON, H. H., 74
WILSON, H. H., 75
WILSON, Hattie O., 74
WILSON, J., 75
WILSON, John B., 75
WILSON, John B., 75
WILSON, John B. jr., 75
WILSON, Joseph Samuel, 26
WILSON, Joshua T., 74
WILSON, Kitty D., 26
WILSON, Nellie R., 75
WILSON, Sarah F., 75
WILSON, Theadore C., 75
WILSON, W. A., 74
WILSON, W. A., 75
WILSON, Willis A., 74
WILSON, Willis A., 74
WILSON, Willis A., 75
WILSON, Willis A., 75
WINFREE, Mary (Mrs.), 45
WINFREE, Nellie Elizabeth (Timberlake), 59
WINKLER, Benton, 39
WINKLER, Mattie, 41
WINKLER, W. A., 41
WOMACK, H., 33
WOMACK, M. B., 33
WOMACK, infant, 33
WOOD, C. (m), 84
WRIGHT, Betty Burford, 41
WRIGHT, David B., 38
WRIGHT, Elizabeth A., 42
WRIGHT, Elizabeth Black, 43
WRIGHT, Harriet, 42
WRIGHT, Hugh Bradley, 43
WRIGHT, James Henry, 62
WRIGHT, Romulus C., 41
WRIGHT, Romulus C., 42
WRIGHT, S. H., 83
WRIGHT, S. H., 84
WRIGHT, S. H., 85
WRIGHT, Sarah Elizabeth, 61
WYATT, Ada B., 76
WYATT, J. G., 76
WYATT, James G., 76
WYATT, John F., 76
WYATT, Johnie W., 76
WYATT, Mary E., 76
WYATT, Sarah A., 76

WYATT, Wm. B., 76
WYATT, Wm. F., 76
YANCY, Fannie Payne, 73
YANCY, W. C., 73
YEAMAN, Minerva F., 77
YEAMAN, N. T., 77
YEARGAN, D., 84
YEARGEN, D., 83
YOUNG, Addison H., 42
YOUNG, Agnes, 42
YOUNG, Agnes Garrett (Mrs.), 38
YOUNG, Cyrus S., 32
YOUNG, Eliza, 16
YOUNG, Elizabeth, 16
YOUNG, Elizabeth A., 42
YOUNG, Elizar, 16
YOUNG, Eunice Roberta, 32
YOUNG, Joseph, 15
YOUNG, Mary Belle, 32
YOUNG, Mary J., 15
YOUNG, Sallie Wright, 42
YOUNG, Sam Martin, 42
YOUNG, Wm. Martin, 42
_____, Abram (black), 100
_____, Aunt Jemima, 37
_____, Bob, 37
_____, Frank (black), 99
_____, Isaac (black), 103
_____, Jewell, 38
_____, Joe (black), 99
_____, Mary (black), 103
_____, Odell, 38
_____, Ottis B., 77
_____, Patt (black f), 99
_____, Priss (black), 94
_____, Stephen (black), 99
_____, Wm. (black), 100